Cross Stitch
TEDDIES

Cross Stitch
TEDDIES

Joan Elliott

D&C
David and Charles

For Dawn and Peter, with love

A note from the author

In the midst of creating this book, the tragic events of 11 September 2001 unfolded before our eyes. In the days that followed, as we all searched for any small form of comfort, I came across an anonymous quote that spoke volumes and reflected the spirit of hope that carries us forward: 'Cuddly and warm, these calming creatures reassure me in days of doubt when fears fly before reason and the world looms bleak instead of beautiful. The Teddy Bear, all things to all ages, all sizes for all preferences, symbol that all could be right with the world, if one only believes.'

A DAVID & CHARLES BOOK
Copyright © David & Charles Limited 2002, 2006

David & Charles is an F+W Publications Inc. company
4700 East Galbraith Road
Cincinnati, OH 45236

First published in the UK in 2002
Reprinted 2003
First paperback edition 2006

Designs, text and decorative artworks
Copyright © Joan Elliott 2002, 2006

The verses used within the book are from anonymous sources except for those on the following pages, which are copyright © Joan Elliott: pages 16, 30, 49, 50, 56, 62, 66, 71, 78, 82, 89, 94, 98.

Joan Elliott has asserted her right to be identified as author of this work in accordance with the Copyright, Designs and Patents Act, 1988.

A catalogue record for this book is available from the British Library.

ISBN-13: 978-0-7153-1196-7 hardback
ISBN-10: 0-7153-1196-4 hardback

ISBN-13: 978-0-7153-2402-8 paperback
ISBN-10: 0-7153-2402-0 paperback

Executive commissioning editor Cheryl Brown
Executive art editor Ali Myer
Book designer Lisa Forrester
Project editor and chart preparation Lin Clements
Photography Lucy Mason
Photographs on pp 37, 71, 83 by Donna Richardson
Copyright © Design Works Crafts 2002

Printed in Singapore by KHL Printing Co Pte Ltd
for David & Charles
Brunel House   Newton Abbot   Devon

Visit our website at www.davidandcharles.co.uk

David & Charles books are available from all good bookshops; alternatively you can contact our Orderline on 0870 9908222 or write to us at FREEPOST EX2 110, D&C Direct, Newton Abbot, TQ12 4ZZ (no stamp required UK only); US customers call 800-289-0963 and Canadian customers call 800-840-5220.

Contents

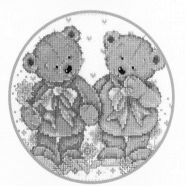

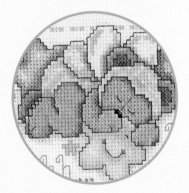

Introduction

The teddy bear has long been a beloved symbol of childhood, its gentle nature transcending gender and age. I remember my own little cinnamon-coloured teddy as a faithful friend. Each summer, he and the other stuffed animals would be washed and hung on the line. I couldn't wait for the afternoon, when my mother would take them down, smelling of warm summer breezes. Loose limbs and tattered paws would be mended and off we'd go, returning to the wonderful world of playful imagination.

It was in 1902 that the 'Teddy' bear as we know it today first emerged. There are disputed versions of its origin, one of which starts in the United States. In November of 1902, President Theodore 'Teddy' Roosevelt journeyed South to settle a border dispute. A famed naturalist and hunter, he took advantage of free time to go on a bear-hunting expedition. To avoid the tangled brush, his guides asked that he wait in a clearing; they would then chase out a bear where he could shoot it. The chase lasted for hours and eventually a bear emerged. The guides tethered the exhausted bear to a tree, but the President thought it unjust to take advantage of the battered creature and refused to shoot.

Political cartoonist Clifford Berryman cleverly depicted the incident, portraying the bear as a bewildered cub.

Seeing the newspaper cartoon, Morris Michtom, proprietor of a sweet shop in Brooklyn, New York, asked his wife Rose to create a jointed stuffed bear, which he displayed in the window. Delighted customers began placing orders. Early in 1903 Michtom wrote to the President asking for permission to call the toy 'Teddy's' bear. Roosevelt granted permission adding that he did not think the name would lend much worth to the toys. From these humble beginnings the Ideal Toy Company began.

Many agree that the name 'Teddy' was rooted in the American legend, however the creation of the first jointed stuffed bear is often attributed to Margarete Steiff. This remarkable woman began the Steiff Toy Company in Germany in 1880. Gaining a reputation for high quality stuffed toys, Richard Steiff, her nephew, thought of offering a stuffed bear for boys as a counterpart to the many dolls available for girls. Sketches presented in 1902 were made up and presented at the Leipzig Toy Fair of 1903. Response from European buyers was mediocre but while the bears were being packed away, a buyer from the United States showed interest and ordered 3,000 on the spot. Whichever story you choose, by 1905 the teddy bear had become the most popular toy world-wide.

It is, indeed, hard to resist the charm of teddy bears. With a twist of their head and a twinkle in their eye, they bring us understanding and love. They express any emotion we need, when we need it. My hope for the designs presented here is that they will bring a smile to your heart and warmth to your home for all to share.

Teddies on a Roll

A TRICYCLE TO COAST ON, a little red wagon filled with toys, a soapbox scooter with baby buggy wheels and teddy bears. These symbols of childhood combine to create a parade of teddies rolling along on a summer outing filled with fun. Fresh green grass tickles their toes and rainbow butterflies come close to see what all the excitement is about. Coloured in their bright pastel shirts and ribbons, they invite us to join the procession. It's a teddy bear line up that's hard to resist.

Teddy Bear, Teddy Bear turn around,
Teddy Bear, Teddy Bear touch the ground,
Teddy Bear, Teddy Bear come and play,
Teddy Bear, Teddy Bear roll away.

Teddies on a Roll

Design Size
58.5 x 20cm (23 x 8in)
Stitch Count
324w x 112h

MATERIALS

70 x 33cm (28 x 13in) antique white 14-count Aida

♥

DMC stranded cotton (floss) as listed in chart key

♥

Tapestry needle number 24

♥

90 x 112cm (36 x 44in) light-weight cotton fabric to tone with embroidery

♥

Matching sewing thread

♥

150cm (60in) decorative braided cord to tone with embroidery

♥

One decorative button

♥

Bolster cushion pad 66cm (26in) long x 20cm (8in) diameter

♥

Two elastic bands

♥

137cm (54in) ribbon 2.5cm (1in) wide to match cord

1 Prepare for work, referring to Techniques. Find and mark the centre of the fabric and mount in a frame if you wish.

2 Start stitching from the centre of the chart and fabric. Use two strands of stranded cotton (floss) for cross stitches and French knots (wound once around the needle), following the chart colour changes. See page 107 for working French knots. Use one strand for the various backstitch outlines. The black backstitch is shown in dark grey on the charts for clarity. Note, some colours use more than one skein.

3 To make up into a bolster cushion cover, take the piece of cotton fabric and use pinking scissors close to all edges. Fold 7.5cm (3in) to the back along one of the long edges and stitch this down 2.5cm (1in) from the fold.

4 With right side up, centre the finished embroidery on the cotton fabric piece and attach it by sewing or fusing (see instructions page 107). Using matching sewing thread, stitch decorative cord around the embroidery, starting and ending at the centre bottom, and stitching the ends together.

(Alternatively, use a thin line of permanent fabric glue, pressing the cord in place.) Attach a decorative button where the cord ends meet.

5 Take a ready-made bolster cushion pad (or see page 108 for instructions on making your own) and place the fabric over it, centring the embroidery. Wrap the fabric around the pad, keeping the long, folded edge over the pinked edge. Gather the fabric at either end and secure with elastic bands. To finish, cut the ribbon in half and wrap and tie each length in bows to hide the elastic bands.

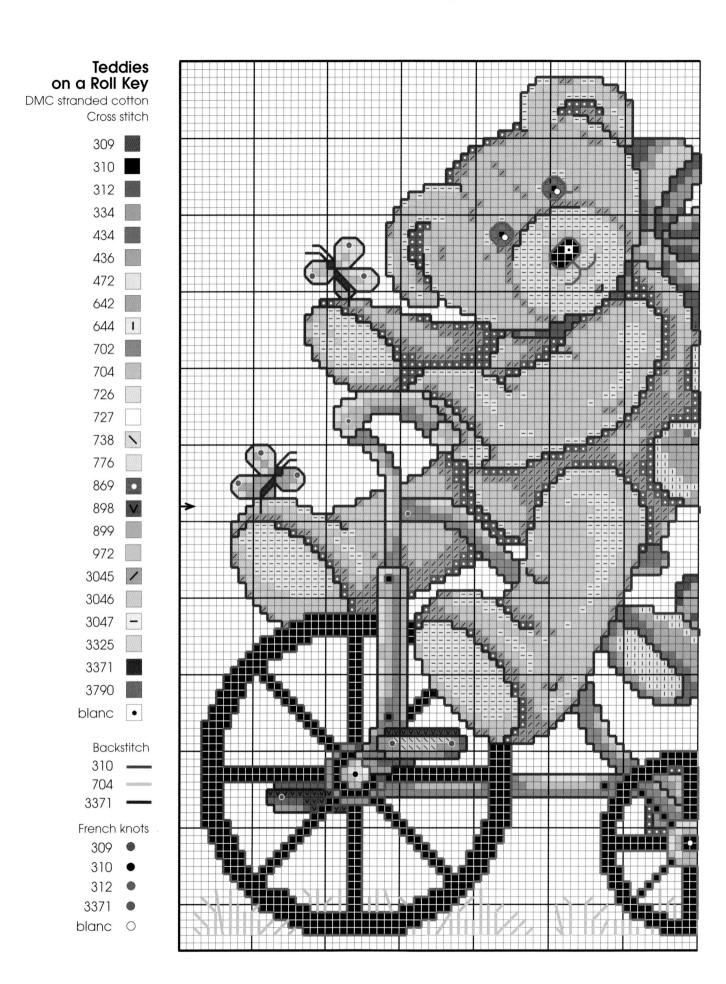

**Teddies
on a Roll Key**

DMC stranded cotton
Cross stitch

309
310
312
334
434
436
472
642
644 |
702
704
726
727
738 \
776
869 ⊙
898 V
899
972
3045 /
3046
3047 −
3325
3371
3790
blanc ⊙

Backstitch
310 ———
704 ———
3371 ———

French knots
309 ●
310 ●
312 ●
3371 ●
blanc ○

12

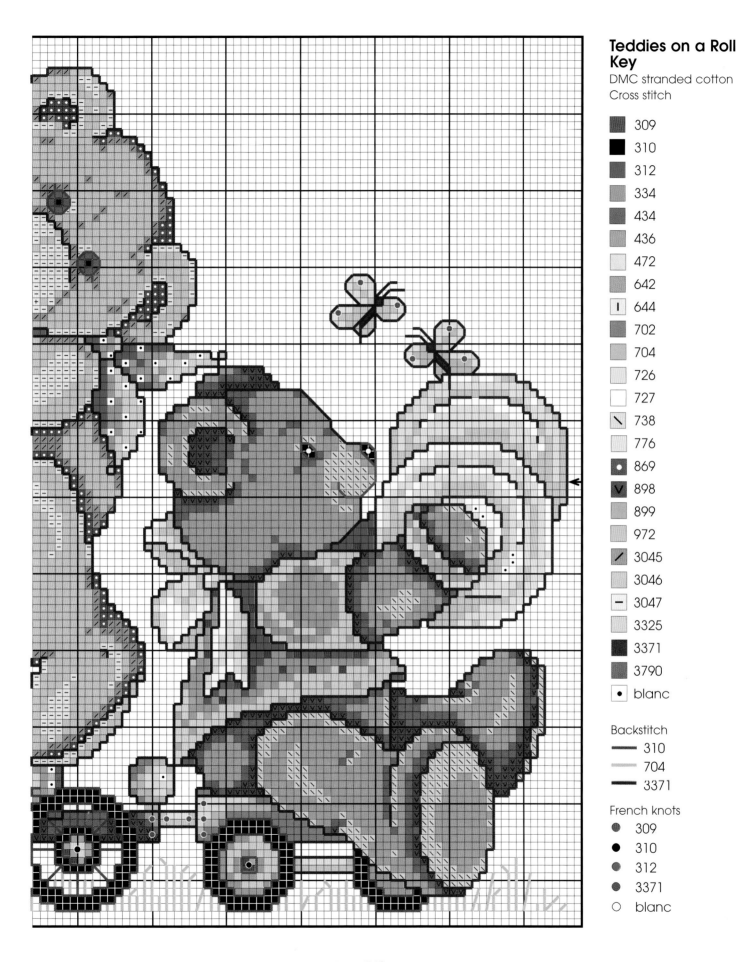

**Teddies on a Roll
Key**

DMC stranded cotton
Cross stitch

▨	309
■	310
▨	312
▨	334
▨	434
▨	436
▨	472
▨	642
I	644
▨	702
▨	704
▨	726
☐	727
\	738
▨	776
◉	869
V	898
▨	899
▨	972
/	3045
▨	3046
−	3047
▨	3325
■	3371
▨	3790
•	blanc

Backstitch
— 310
— 704
— 3371

French knots
● 309
● 310
● 312
● 3371
○ blanc

15

Julie's Kitchen

THE KITCHEN IS A GATHERING PLACE filled with warmth, love of home and the wonderful aromas of good food. Dressed in chef's hat and apron, this teddy is mixing up a delicious surprise. Brighten your kitchen and keep your recipes close at hand with this charming book cover. The kitchen ensemble also includes a potholder for removing hot apple pie from the oven, a kitchen towel for tidying up and a set of four jar lid covers to top off your home-made jams.

Come into my kitchen,
What's that I hear you say?
Come and tell us all the news
you've heard 'round town today.

A little conversation,
Perhaps a cup of tea?
Come and spend a lovely time
with Teddy Bear and me.

Recipe Book Cover

Design Size
15 x 20cm (6 x 8in)
Stitch Count
98w x 126h

MATERIALS
28 x 33cm (11 x 13in) antique white 16-count Aida

♥

DMC stranded cotton (floss) as listed in chart key

♥

Tapestry needle number 24

♥

15 x 20cm (6 x 8in) white cotton batting (wadding) or felt

1 Prepare for work, referring to Techniques. Find and mark the centre of the fabric and mount in a frame if you wish.

2 Start stitching from the centre of the chart and fabric, using two strands of stranded cotton (floss) for the cross stitches and French knots (wound once around the needle), following the colours on the chart. Work the backstitches using one strand.

3 Stitch the name of your choice by copying the letters you need from the charted alphabet on to grid paper. Find the centre of your name on the grid and the centre of the name space on the fabric and begin stitching from

the centre outwards using two strands of 792 for the cross stitch and the backstitch apostrophe.

4 When the stitching is complete, trim the embroidery to within twelve rows of the design. Fold over the edges by eight rows, leaving four rows showing around the design and press into place. To avoid the background fabric showing through the embroidery, cut a piece of thin cotton wadding (batting) or felt the same size as the design and insert it behind the embroidery.

5 Your embroidery is now ready to be mounted on a fabric-covered binder – see page 107 for the materials needed and the technique.

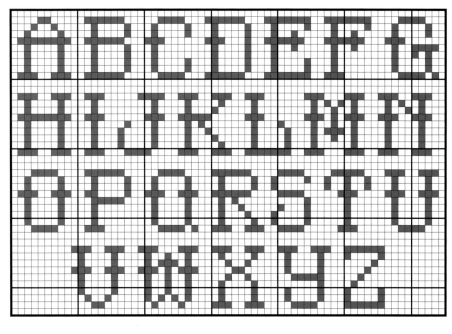

Recipe Book Cover Key
DMC stranded cotton
Cross stitch

■ 310	▨ 792	– 3078
▨ 318	▨ 793	▨ 3705
■ 321	▨ 794	V 3706
▨ 414	I 828	▨ 3708
╱ 415	▨ 869	• blanc
▨ 553	▨ 904	**Backstitch**
▨ 554	▨ 906	—— 310
╲ 677	▨ 907	—— 792
▨ 726	▨ 3045	**French knots**
▨ 742	▨ 3046	● 310
		● 904

Kitchen Towel

Design Size
40 x 14cm (4 x 5½in)

Stitch Count
56w x 76h

MATERIALS

Charles Craft Showcase Huck towel (#HF-6500-2724 – see Suppliers), in ecru with a 14-count insert

♥

DMC stranded cotton (floss) as listed in chart key

♥

Tapestry needle number 24

1 Find and mark the centre of the towel insert and the centre of the chart. Start stitching from the centre outwards using two strands of stranded cotton (floss) for the cross stitches and the French knots (wound once around the needle). Use one strand for all the backstitches.

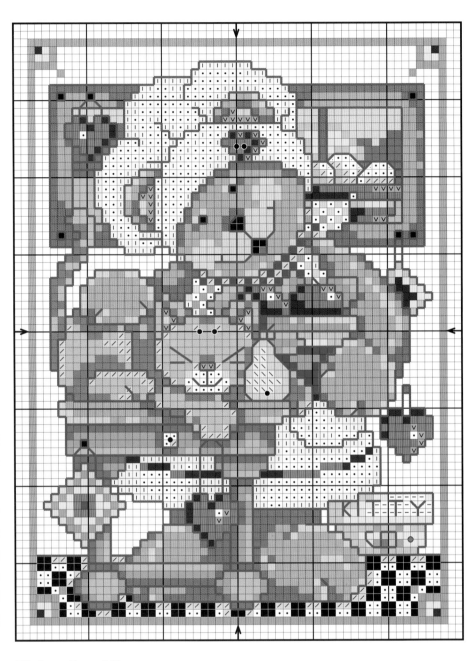

Kitchen Towel Key
DMC stranded cotton
Cross stitch

■ 310	▨ 553	▨ 792	▨ 904	− 3078	▨ 3705	**Backstitch**	
▨ 318	▨ 554	▨ 793	▨ 906		▨ 3705	—— 310	
■ 321	＼ 677	794	907	V 3706			
▨ 414	▨ 726	I 828	▨ 3045	▨ 3708	**French knots**	
╱ 415	▨ 742	▨ 869	▨ 3046	• blanc	● 310	● 904

Potholder

Design Size
14 x 10cm (5½ x 4in)

Stitch Count
76w x 57h

MATERIALS
Charles Craft Kitchen Mates™ potholder (#PH-6201-2724 – see Suppliers), in ecru with a 14-count insert

♥

DMC stranded cotton (floss) as listed in chart key

♥

Tapestry needle number 24

1 Open part of the outside seam on the potholder, freeing the Aida insert for easier access.

2 Start stitching from the centre, using two strands of stranded cotton (floss) for cross stitches and French knots (wound once around the needle) and one strand for backstitches. Re-stitch the seam when finished.

Potholder Key
DMC stranded cotton
Cross stitch

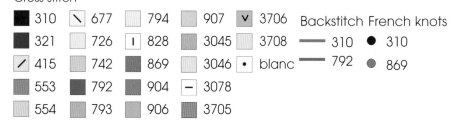

					Backstitch	French knots
■ 310	＼ 677	794	907	∨ 3706		
321	726	Ⅰ 828	3045	3708	— 310	● 310
／ 415	742	869	3046	• blanc	— 792	● 869
553	792	904	− 3078			
554	793	906	3705			

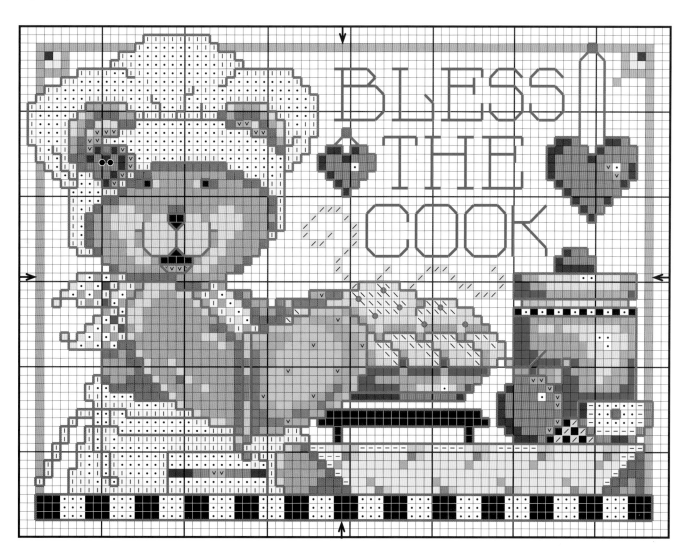

Jar Lid Covers

Design Size (for each lid)
6 x 6cm (2¼ x 2¼in)
Stitch Count
43w x 43h

MATERIALS (for each lid)
18 x 18cm (7 x 7in) antique
white 18-count Aida

♥

DMC stranded cotton (floss)
as listed in chart key

♥

Tapestry needle number 24

♥

1m (1yd) ribbon ⅝in wide to
tone with embroidery

♥

18cm (7in) elastic 1.25cm
(½in) wide

♥

Matching sewing thread

♥

Decorative bow

1 Start stitching from the centre of the fabric pieces following the charts, using two strands of stranded cotton (floss) for cross stitches and French knots (wound once around the needle) and one strand for backstitching.

2 Using the charted alphabet and one strand of 310, back-stitch the name of your choice (first planning it on grid paper as described in step 3 of the recipe book cover).

3 Once stitching is complete, trim the fabric 4cm (1½in) from the edge of the stitching, creating a 14cm (5½in) square. Carefully pull out four rows of threads on each edge to create a fringe.

4 To make an elastic ribbon band, cut the ribbon into two 46cm (18in) lengths. Sew the cut ends under by 6mm (¼in). Stitch the two pieces of ribbon together along both long edges, close to the edge. Feed the elastic through the ribbon casing (attach a safety pin to the elastic to pull through), gathering the ribbon as you go. Stitch the ends of the elastic together, easing the ribbon around the elastic until it is completely hidden, then tack (baste) the edges of the ribbon together. Glue or sew a matching bow to the ribbon band at the bottom centre of the design. Centre the embroidery on the jar lid and secure with the elastic ribbon.

Jar Lid Covers Key

DMC stranded cotton
Cross stitch

■ 310	■ 553	□ 726	794	■ 904	■ 3045	＼ 3706
■ 321	554	■ 792	／ 828	■ 906	■ 3046	3708
– 415	I 677	793	■ 869	907	■ 3705	• blanc

Backstitch —— 310
French knots ● 310

A Cuddle of Teddies

AMIDST THE DAY-TO-DAY HUSTLE AND BUSTLE, this picture of teddy bears snuggled up against a fluffy pillow can remind us to slow down and pay attention to the softer side of life. Surrounded by miniature rose-buds and decorative pillows, this endearing collection of teddies is just waiting to lend an ear. No matter what their size or colour – cinnamon, honey or dusty brown – a teddy's arms are always ready to give a hug just when it's most needed.

Design Size
41 x 30cm (16 x 12in)
Stitch Count
224w x 167h

MATERIALS
53 x 43cm (21 x 17in) antique white 14-count Aida

♥

DMC stranded cotton (floss) as listed in chart key

♥

Tapestry needle number 24

1 Prepare for work, referring to Techniques. Mark the centre of the fabric and mount in a frame if you wish. The chart is quite detailed so it would help to enlarge it on a colour photocopier.

2 Start stitching from the centre of the chart and fabric, working all cross stitches using two strands of stranded cotton (floss). Please note that some colours use more than one skein. Work the various French knots using two strands wound once around the needle, according to the colour changes on the chart. Work all backstitch outlines using one strand of 310 (shown in grey on the chart).

3 Once stitching is complete, finish your picture by mounting and framing (see page 108).

*Learn to Listen like
the Teddy Bears –
With ears open and
mouths closed tight.
Learn to Forgive
like the Teddy Bears –
With hearts wide open,
no matter who's right.
Learn to Love
like the Teddy Bears –
With arms wide open and
no end in sight.*

24

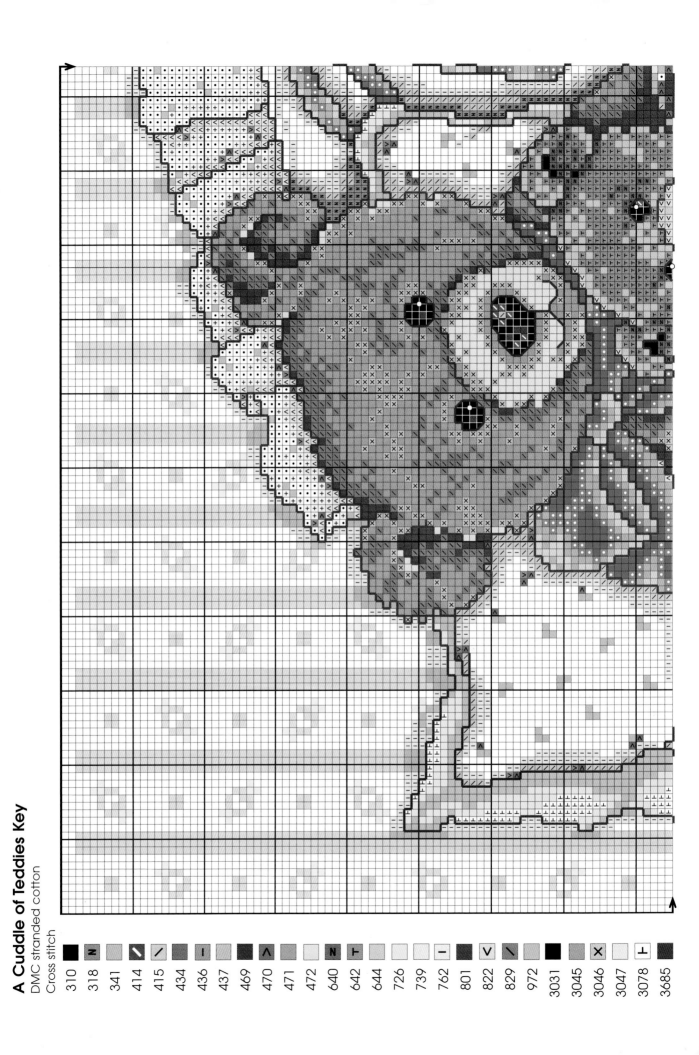

A Cuddle of Teddies Key
DMC stranded cotton
Cross stitch

| | 310 | | 318 | | 341 | | 414 | | 415 | | 434 | | 436 | | 437 | | 469 | | 470 | | 471 | | 472 | | 640 | | 642 | | 644 | | 726 | | 739 | | 762 | | 801 | | 822 | | 829 | | 972 | | 3031 | | 3045 | | 3046 | | 3047 | | 3078 | | 3685 |

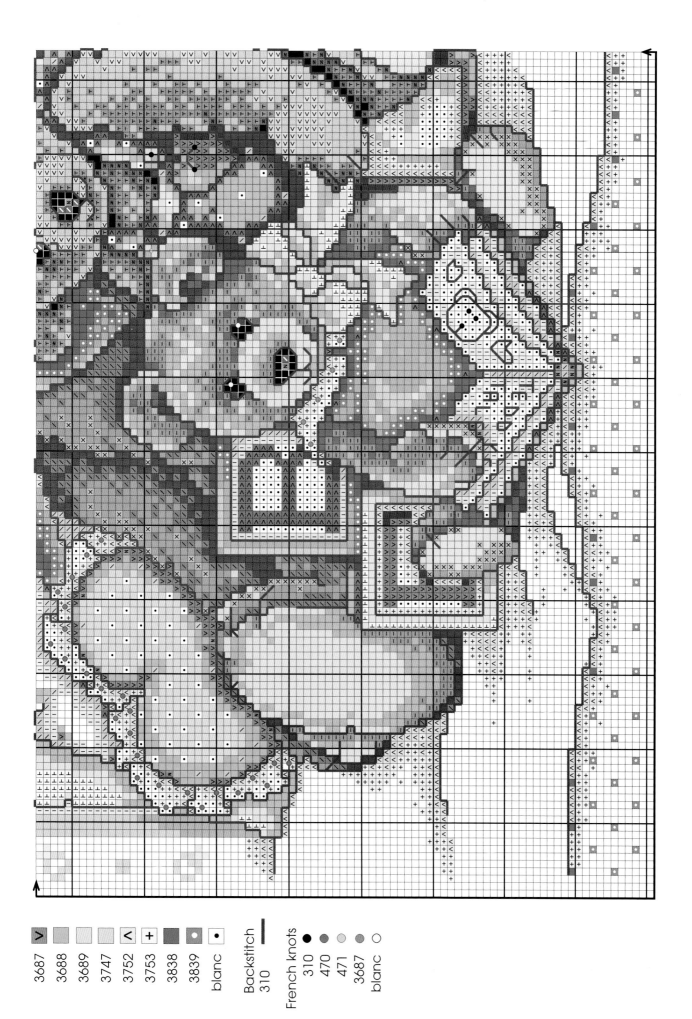

3687
3688
3689
3747
3752
3753
3838
3839
blanc

Backstitch
310

French knots
310
470
471
3687
blanc

A Cuddle of Teddies Key

DMC stranded cotton
Cross stitch

	Colour
■	310
N	318
	341
╲	414
╱	415
	434
I	436
	437
∧	469
	470
N	471
⊤	472
	640
	642
	644
	726
	739
—	762
	801
V	822
╲	829
	972
■	3031
	3045
X	3046
	3047
⊤	3078
■	3685

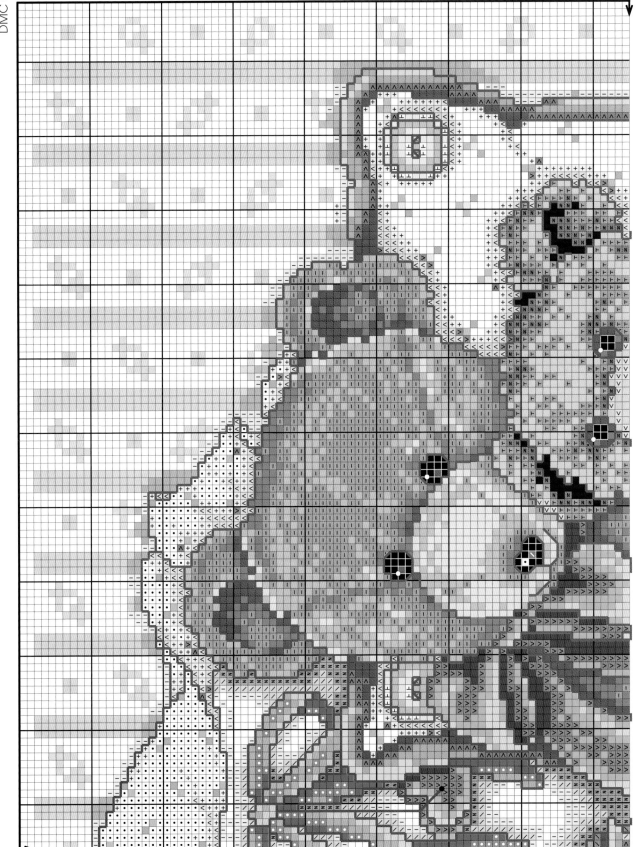

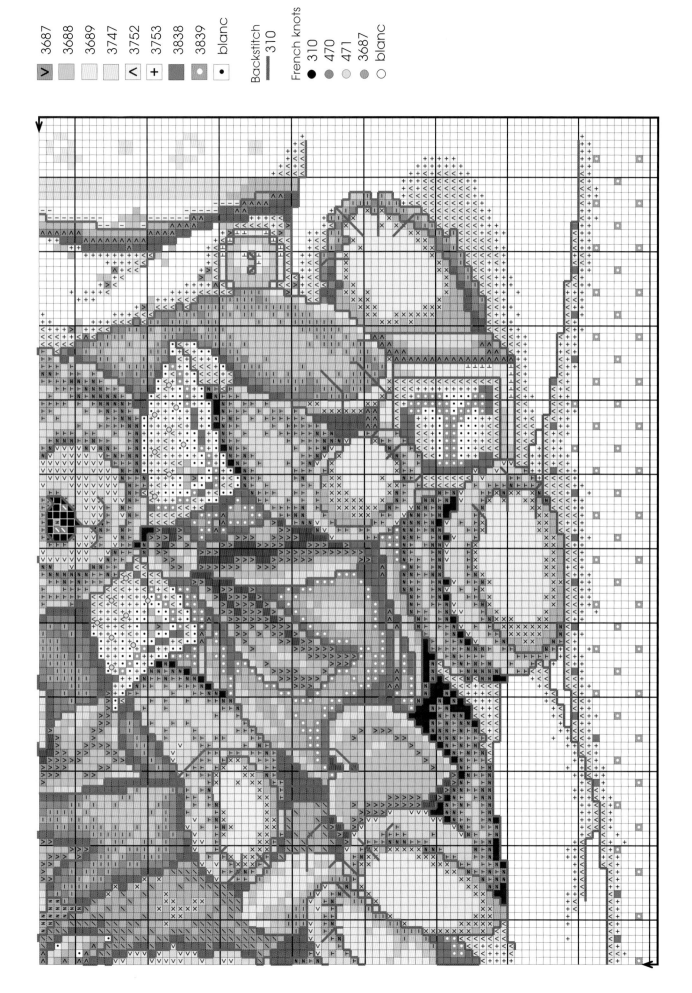

Patchwork Bears

THIS PATCHWORK BEAR may seem torn and tattered but a few small stitches will mend him right up, ready to be hugged and squeezed and then mended once again. Reflecting the country charm of quilts and samplers, calicos and gingham, this teddy work box will hold all your sewing essentials. Place your pins in safe keeping on the little teddy sampler pincushion and tuck your needles safely away in the needlecase.

Sewing Box

Design Size
23 x 16.5cm (9 x 6½in)
Stitch Count
127w x 90h

MATERIALS
36 x 28cm (14 x 11in) Fiddler's Light 14-count Aida

♥

DMC stranded cotton (floss) as listed in chart key

♥

Tapestry needle number 24

♥

Shaker oval box (Sudberry House #99671 – see Suppliers)

♥

76cm (30in) decorative piping to tone with embroidery

♥

Fabric glue

1 Prepare for work, referring to Techniques. Find and then mark the centre of the fabric and mount in a frame if you wish.

2 Start stitching from the centre of the chart and fabric, using two strands of stranded cotton (floss) for cross stitches and French knots (wound once around the needle). Use one strand for backstitches.

3 Once complete, mount in the box top following the manufacturer's instructions. Add a decorative edge by gluing the piping close to the edge of the mounted embroidery. Overlap the two ends and glue the raw edges to the back.

My Teddy may be worn out,
but never shall we part,
What is it about him that
touches so my heart?

His seams are always tearing
and soon need to be sewn,
But he is still my best friend,
whenever I'm alone.

His ears are loose and floppy,
his paw pads need repair,
But it doesn't really matter,
for he's my Teddy Bear.

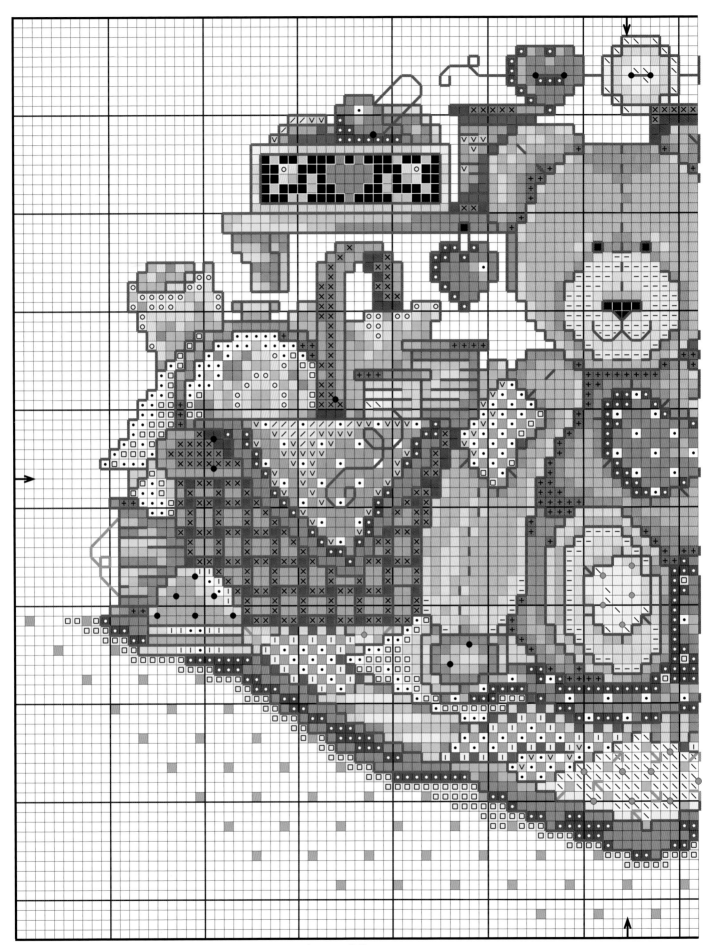

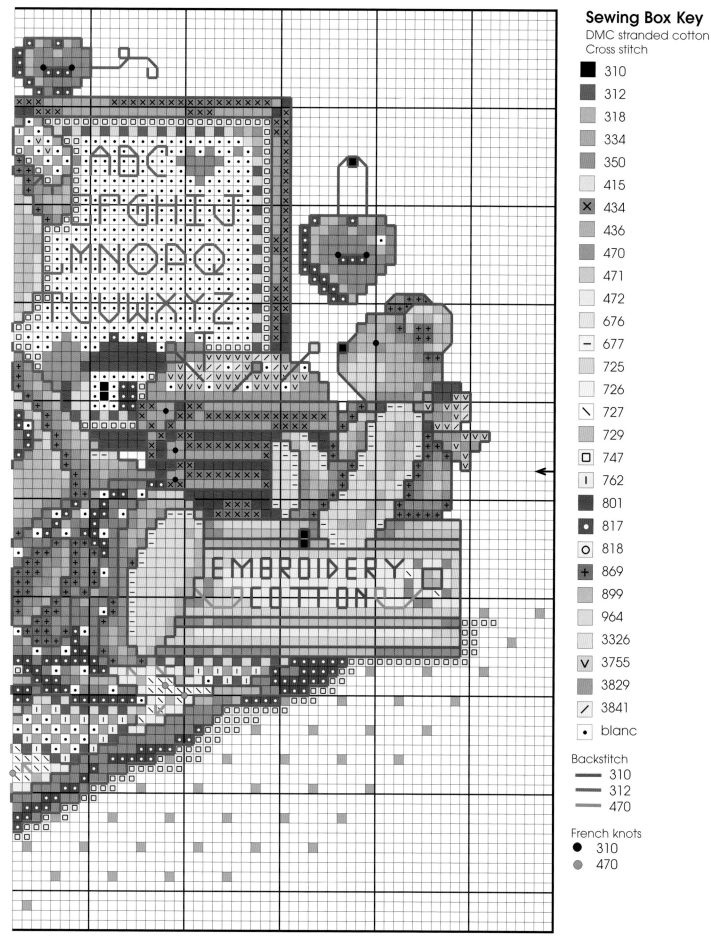

Sewing Box Key

DMC stranded cotton
Cross stitch

■	310
	312
	318
	334
	350
	415
✕	434
	436
	470
	471
	472
	676
−	677
	725
	726
＼	727
	729
☐	747
Ⅰ	762
	801
⊡	817
⊙	818
＋	869
	899
	964
	3326
Ⅴ	3755
	3829
／	3841
•	blanc

Backstitch

═══ 310
═══ 312
═══ 470

French knots
● 310
● 470

Design Size
7.5 x 7.5cm (3 x 3in)
Stitch Count
55w x 55h

MATERIALS

20 x 20cm (8 x 8in) Fiddler's Light 18-count Aida

♥

DMC stranded cotton (floss) as listed in chart key

♥

Tapestry needle number 24

♥

13 x 13cm (5 x 5in) lightweight iron-on interfacing

♥

46cm (18in) decorative piping to tone with embroidery

♥

13 x 13cm (5 x 5in) backing fabric to tone with embroidery

♥

Matching sewing thread

♥

Polyester filling

Pincushion and Needlecase Key
DMC stranded cotton
Cross stitch

■ 310	472	◉ 817
312	676	○ 818
318	– 677	✛ 869
334	725	899
350	726	964
415	╲ 727	3326
✕ 434	729	V 3755
436	▢ 747	3829
470	I 762	╱ 3841
471	■ 801	• blanc

Backstitch
— 310
— 312
— 470

French knots
● 310
● 470

Pincushion

1 Prepare for work, finding and then marking the centre of the fabric. Follow the stitching instructions in step 2 of the sewing box on page 30.

2 Make up into a pincushion by trimming the finished embroidery, leaving twelve rows beyond the design edges. Cut iron-on interfacing to the same size and iron on to the wrong side of the embroidery.

3 Starting at centre bottom, tack (baste) the piping to the right side, raw edges matching, six rows from the design. Now cut the backing fabric to the same size as the trimmed embroidery and pin in place, right sides facing. Stitch a 1.25cm (½in) seam all round, leaving an opening for turning at the bottom edge. Turn through and stuff with polyester filling. Tuck in the piping at the opening and slipstitch closed.

Needlecase

1 Fold the Aida in half and with the fold to the left, centre the design on the top half. Start stitching from the centre, using two strands of stranded cotton (floss) for cross stitches and French knots (wound twice around the needle). Work the backstitches with one strand.

2 When the embroidery is complete make up into a needlecase. Press carefully and with a soft pencil draw a 8.25 x 15cm (3¼ x 6in) rectangle leaving twelve rows around the top, bottom and right side of the stitched area. Cut away excess fabric along the pencil lines.

3 To attach the bias binding, pin it along all four edges, right side facing, raw edges matching. Stitch the tape five rows from the finished design. Place the embroidery wrong side up and iron on the interfacing. Turn the binding down and over to the wrong side to form the edging, slipstitching in place through the interfacing.

4 With the inside facing up, layer one piece of fusible web, the two ribbons with their ends placed 1.25cm (½in) in from the centre of each short edge, one piece of felt, another piece of fusible web, and the second piece of felt. Press and fuse all securely. Fold the case in half and tie the ribbons in a bow.

Design Size
5 x 5cm (2 x 2in)
Stitch Count
38w x 37h

MATERIALS

25 x 18cm (10 x 7in) Fiddler's Light 18-count Aida

♥

DMC stranded cotton (floss) as listed in chart key

♥

Tapestry needle number 24

♥

60cm (24in) bias binding 2.5cm (1in) wide to tone with embroidery

♥

9 x 15cm (3½ x 6in) iron-on interfacing

♥

Two 9 x 14cm (3½ x 5½in) pieces of felt

♥

Two 9 x 14cm (3½ x 5½in) pieces of fusible web (Steam-a-Seam2)

♥

Two 15cm (6in) lengths of ⅛in wide ribbon to tone

♥

Matching sewing thread

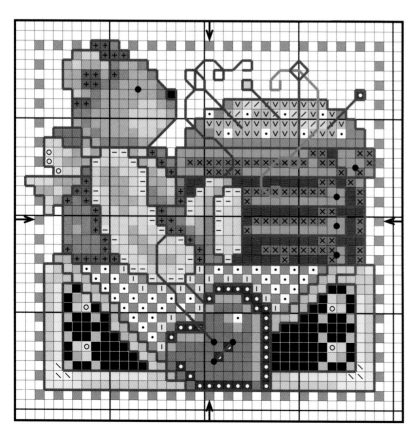

Baby Bear's Arrival

IT SEEMS FITTING THAT THE TEDDY BEAR has come to hold the qualities we most cherish in childhood. Cuddly, soft and loving, we often choose a teddy as the first present for a newborn. This darling bear sits in front of a country quilt of hearts and flowers. Embroidered on his pyjama top is a loving heart. The picture has a gentle palette of baby-soft pastels to blend beautifully in any nursery. Add baby's name and birth date using the alphabet provided to create a lasting remembrance of this joyous event.

Design Size
18 x 23cm (7 x 9in)
Stitch Count
98w x 126h

MATERIALS
30 x 36cm (12 x 14in) white
14-count Aida

♥

DMC stranded cotton (floss)
as listed in chart key

♥

Tapestry needle number 24

1   Prepare for work, referring to Techniques. Find and mark the centre of the fabric and mount in an embroidery frame if you wish.

2   Start stitching from the centre of the chart and fabric, working all cross stitches using two strands of stranded cotton (floss). Work French knots (wound once around the needle) in two strands of white (blanc) in the bear's eyes and in 3371 in the bunnies' eyes and on their sleeves. Backstitch all outlines using one strand of 3371.

3   Copy the letters and numbers for the name and birth date from the alphabet chart on to grid paper. Find the centre of your grid and the centre of the space on the embroidery and begin stitching from the centre out, using two strands of blue 334.

4   Once stitching is complete, finish your picture by mounting and framing (see page 108).

WILLIAM MICHAEL
JANUARY 26, 1997

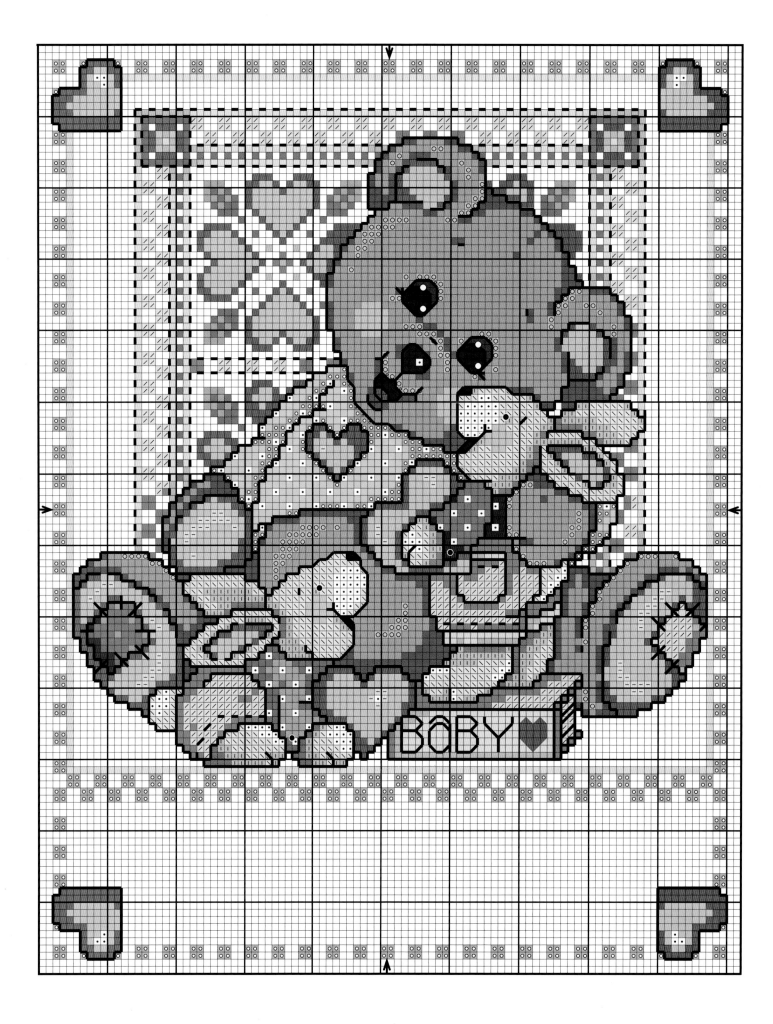

Baby Bear's Arrival Key

DMC stranded cotton
Cross stitch

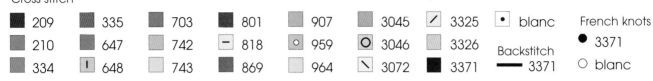

■ 209	▨ 335	▨ 703	■ 801	▨ 907	▨ 3045	⁄ 3325	• blanc		French knots			
■ 210	▨ 647	▨ 742	− 818	⊙ 959	⦿ 3046		3326		● 3371			
■ 334	∣ 648	743	■ 869	964	＼ 3072	■ 3371	Backstitch	─ 3371	○ blanc			

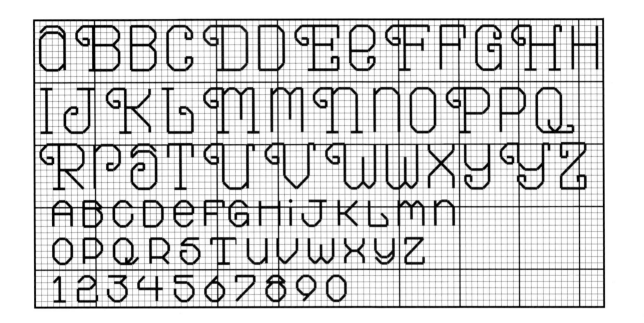

When I was only four days old
You came to live with me,
And gave me all the love you hold
Quite unreservedly.

Oh Teddy Bear I still love thee
As much as I did then,
Though now we both are forty-three
And very nearly men.

Sweet Dream Teddies

TEDDY BEARS ARE the perfect symbol of childhood. Worked in the softest colours, this cosy cot blanket will send your little one off to slumber under a cover of smiling stars and loving hearts. Angelic baby bears alight beside their honey-sweet friend. Let everyone know that it's naptime by placing the door hanger outside baby's room. When baby wakes, tie on one of the pastel gingham-trimmed bibs. A soft block adorned with angel bears fresh from heaven makes the perfect plaything. This ensemble also makes a welcoming gift for a new arrival.

One of the angel designs from the Soft Block decorates a baby's bib beautifully. The one shown here is from Charles Craft (#BB-3650-5640 – see Suppliers) but you could hand stitch the embroidery on to the front of any bib or T-shirt. Follow the chart on page 47 and the stitching details in step 1 of the Soft Block on page 43. The angel motifs could also be made up into charming greetings cards.

Cot Blanket

Design Sizes

Central design:
42 x 53cm (16½ x 21in)
Border stars:
6.5 x 6cm (2½ x 2¼in)
Border hearts:
7 x 6.5cm (2¾ x 2½in)

Stitch Counts

Central design: 149w x 189h
Border stars: 23w x 21h
Border hearts: 25w x 22h

MATERIALS

Baby Alphabet Afghan antique white 18-count (Charles Craft, AF 7311-0322, see Suppliers)

♥

DMC stranded cotton (floss) as listed in chart key

♥

Tapestry needle number 24

1 Prepare for work, referring to Techniques. Mark the centre of the central Afghan panel and start stitching from the centre of the chart (pages 44/45), working cross stitches over two threads using three strands. Note, some colours use more than one skein. The variously coloured French knots use three strands wound once around the needle. Work the backstitches of all eyes, noses, and mouths using two strands of 310. Work the 'strings' on the stars and hearts using two strands of 912. Work the backstitches on the tiny stars using one strand of 972 and the clouds in 334. Work other backstitches with one strand of 938.

2 For the border, stitch the hearts and stars (charts page 46) in the centres of the Afghan border squares, as shown in this diagram. The red lines show the Afghan squares.

3 Once stitching is complete, fringe the edges of the blanket by finding the raised threads on the outer edge, removing the threads on all sides leaving four threads remaining beyond the raised area. Starting at a corner, count off ten thread ends and tie in a knot, pushing it up close to the raised threads. Continue this all round.

Alternatively, create an unknotted fringe by running a machine stitch around the outer edge of the blanket four rows beyond the raised threads. Trim the blanket to within 5cm (2in) of the machine stitching and remove the threads up to the stitching line.

Soft Block

Design Size
(for each design)
9 x 9cm (3½ x 3½in)
Stitch Count
49w x 48h

MATERIALS
Six 20 x 20cm (8 x 8in) squares antique white 14-count Aida

♥

DMC stranded cotton (floss) as listed in chart key

♥

Tapestry needle number 24

♥

Matching sewing thread

♥

0.5 x 1m (½ x 1yd) medium-weight iron-on interfacing

♥

Polyester stuffing

1   Find and mark the centre of each of the six fabric squares. There are three motifs – two angel bears and a large pink heart and you will need to stitch two of each. Start stitching from the centre of the charts (on pages 46/47) in the centre of each fabric piece, using two strands of stranded cotton (floss) for cross stitches and French knots (wound once around the needle). Work the backstitches for the 'strings' using two strands of 912. Work the other variously coloured backstitches using one strand.

2   Once stitching is complete, make up into a block. Trim each embroidery leaving fourteen rows beyond the design edges. Cut a piece of iron-on interfacing the same size as the finished square and press on to the wrong side. Repeat for all six squares.

3   Using one heart square as a base, pin and tack (baste) an angel square on to each of the four edges of this base, right sides facing and all four teddies facing in the same direction. Using matching sewing thread, stitch the seams with a 1.25cm (½in) allowance, then press open. Fold each square upwards, sides meeting, right sides facing, and stitch the matching sides together. To finish the cube, pin and tack (baste) the remaining square in place, then stitch along three edges, leaving one open. Taking care to remove all pins, turn the block right side out and fill with stuffing. Slipstitch the gap closed.

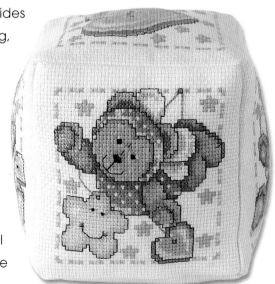

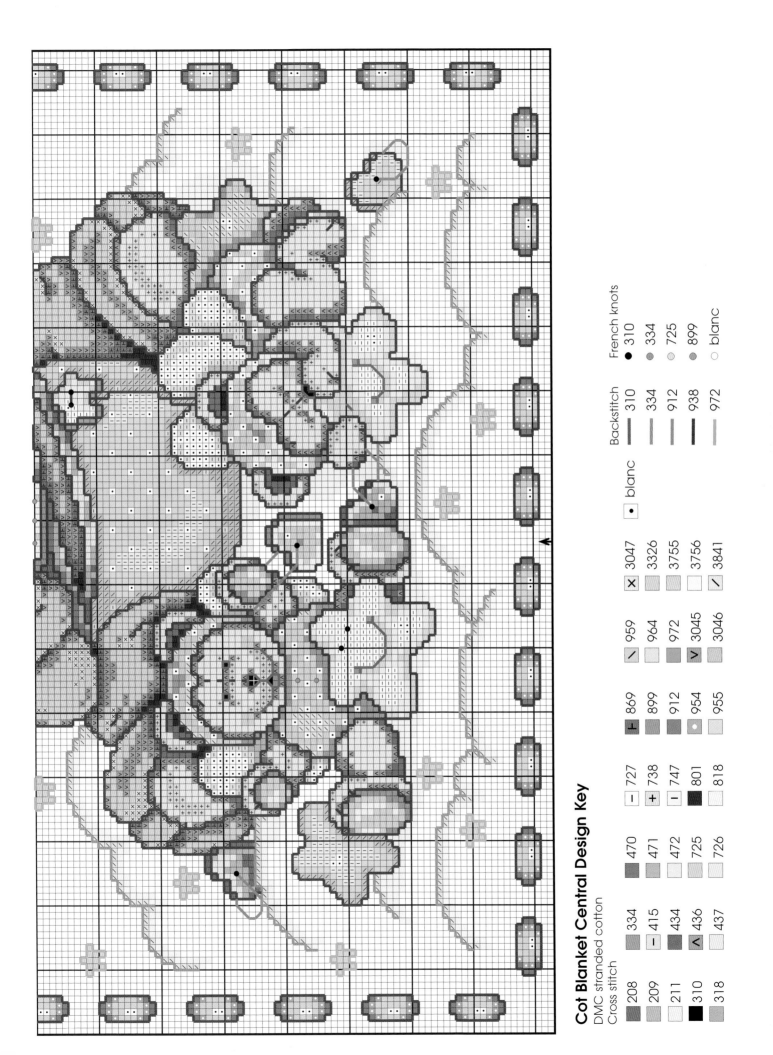

Cot Blanket Central Design Key

DMC stranded cotton
Cross stitch

	208		334		727
	209	–	415	+	738
	211		434	—	747
	310	∧	436		725
	318		437		726

	869		959		blanc
	899	∕	964	·	
	912		972		
	954	∨	3045		
	955		3046		

×	3047
	3326
	3755
	3756
∕	3841

Backstitch
—	310
—	334
—	912
—	938
—	972

French knots
●	310
●	334
●	725
●	899
○	blanc

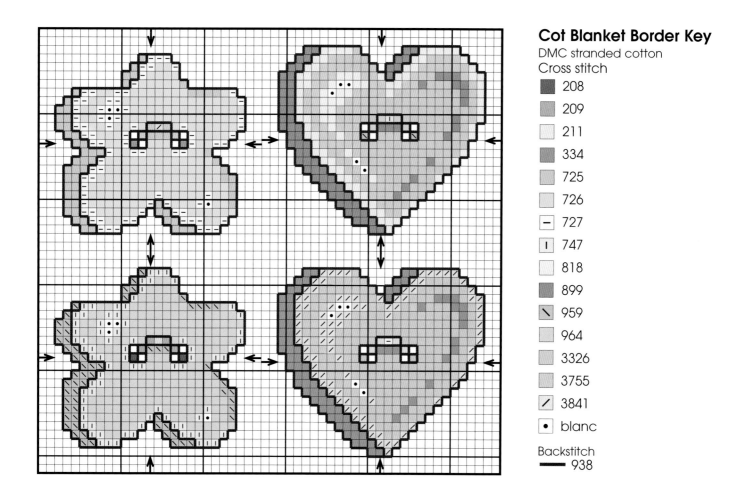

Cot Blanket Border Key

DMC stranded cotton
Cross stitch

- 208
- 209
- 211
- 334
- 725
- 726
- — 727
- | 747
- 818
- 899
- \ 959
- 964
- 3326
- 3755
- / 3841
- • blanc

Backstitch
— 938

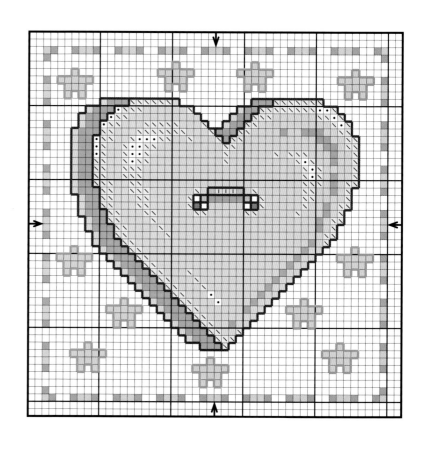

Soft Block Key

DMC stranded cotton
Cross stitch

208	
209	
211	
310	
318	
334	
415	V
434	
436	○
437	
725	
726	/
727	
738	–
801	
818	\
899	
954	
955	
3326	
3755	
3756	
3841	I
blanc	•

Backstitch

310	
912	
938	
972	

French knots

310	●
725	○
899	○

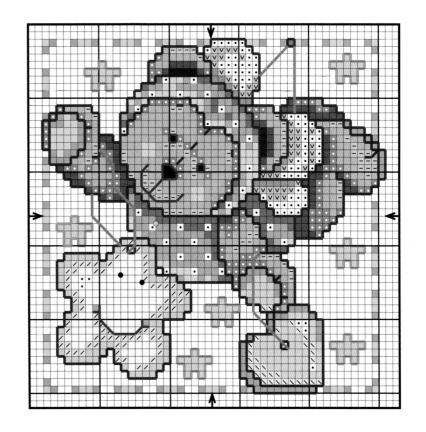

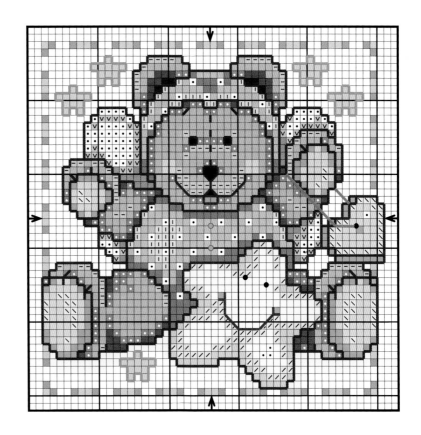

Door Plate

Design Size
14 x 9cm (5½ x 3½in)
Stitch Count
76w x 48h

MATERIALS

25 x 20cm (10 x 8in) antique white 14-count Aida

♥

DMC stranded cotton (floss) as listed in chart key

♥

Tapestry needle number 24

♥

15 x 10cm (6 x 4in) heavy white card

♥

Two 13 x 18cm (5 x 7in) pieces of medium-weight, iron-on interfacing

♥

Two 13 x 18cm (5 x 7in) pieces of pale yellow felt

♥

Fusible web (Steam-a-Seam2, see Suppliers)

♥

38cm (15in) length of ¼in wide ribbon

♥

Permanent fabric glue

1 Prepare for work, referring to Techniques. Find and mark the centre of the fabric and start stitching from the centre of the chart, using two strands of stranded cotton (floss) for cross stitches and French knots (wound once around the needle). Work the backstitch using two strands of 912 for the 'strings' and one strand for all other outlines, following the chart colour changes.

2 Once stitching is complete make up into a door plate as follows. Trim the embroidery ten rows beyond the design. Fold the edges to the back leaving a four-row border all around. Press the folds. Trim the heavy card to fit behind the embroidery under the folded edges. Glue the edges to the back of the card with permanent fabric glue.

3 Iron a piece of iron-on interfacing on to each piece of felt. Place one piece of felt interfacing side up and cut a piece of fusible web to match the felt size. Place this on top then add the second piece of felt, interfacing side down. Using a press cloth, iron to fuse the layers, leaving the top edge open.

4 For a decorative effect, use pinking shears all around the felt close to the edge. Position the two lengths of ribbon, each 4cm (1½in) from the side edges of the felt, inserting 2.5cm (1in) between the layers. Iron to fuse the top edge.

5 Apply permanent fabric glue sparingly to the back of the embroidery close to the edge. Carefully position the embroidery on the felt leaving an equal border all around, making sure no glue oozes out. Tie the ribbons in a bow to create a hanger.

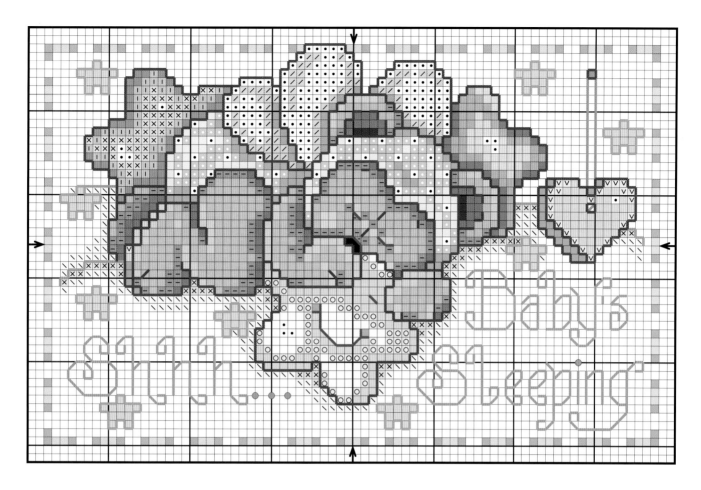

Door Plate Key

DMC stranded cotton
Cross stitch

208	318	– 436	727	✓ 818	959	＼ 3756		
209	334	437	738	899	○ 964	✕ 3841		
211	╱ 415	725	747	954	3326	• blanc		
310	434	○ 726	801	955	3755			

Backstitch
— 310
— 334
— 912
— 938
— 972

French knots
● 334

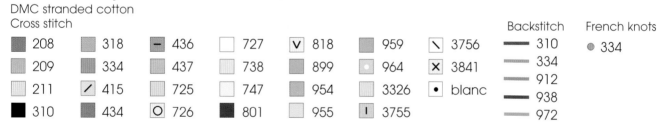

Go to sleep my Teddy Bear,
Close your button eyes.
Let me smooth your silky hair
Beneath the starry skies.

I'd love to cuddle down by you,
And dream the whole night through.
So go to sleep my Teddy Bear
And I will stay with you.

Granny Bear's Memories

THE SWEET SONG OF LAUGHTER, the cosy pleasure of a bedtime story and the wonder of life that exists in every child are only part of the many blessings that grandchildren bring. Whether they are little tots or already grown, you'll want to preserve the precious memories of your time spent together. This easily made photograph album is the perfect way to hold on to those treasured moments and what fun it will be to have on hand as the children grow. Grandchildren truly do make life wonderful!

Design Size
18 x 23cm (7 x 9in)
Stitch Count
98w x 126h

MATERIALS
30 x 36cm (12 x 14in) white
14-count Aida

♥

DMC stranded cotton (floss)
as listed in chart key

♥

Tapestry needle number 24

♥

18 x 23cm (7 x 9in) white
cotton wadding (batting)
or felt

1 Prepare for work, referring to Techniques. Find and mark the centre of the fabric and mount in a frame if you wish.

2 Start stitching from the centre of the chart and fabric, using two strands of stranded cotton (floss) for the cross stitches and French knots (wound once around the needle). Work the backstitch outlines using one strand.

3 When stitching is complete, trim to within twelve rows of the design. Fold over the edges by eight rows leaving four rows showing around the design. Press into place. To avoid the background fabric showing through

the embroidery, cut a piece of thin cotton wadding (batting) or felt the same size as the design and insert it behind the embroidery.

4 Mount the embroidery on a fabric-covered binder – see page 107 for materials and technique.

Come here dearest children,
Come see what I have found!
Granny has a special treat,
so Teddies gather 'round.

It is a book of memories,
Of sweet and gentle love.
For you are all a special gift,
A blessing from above.

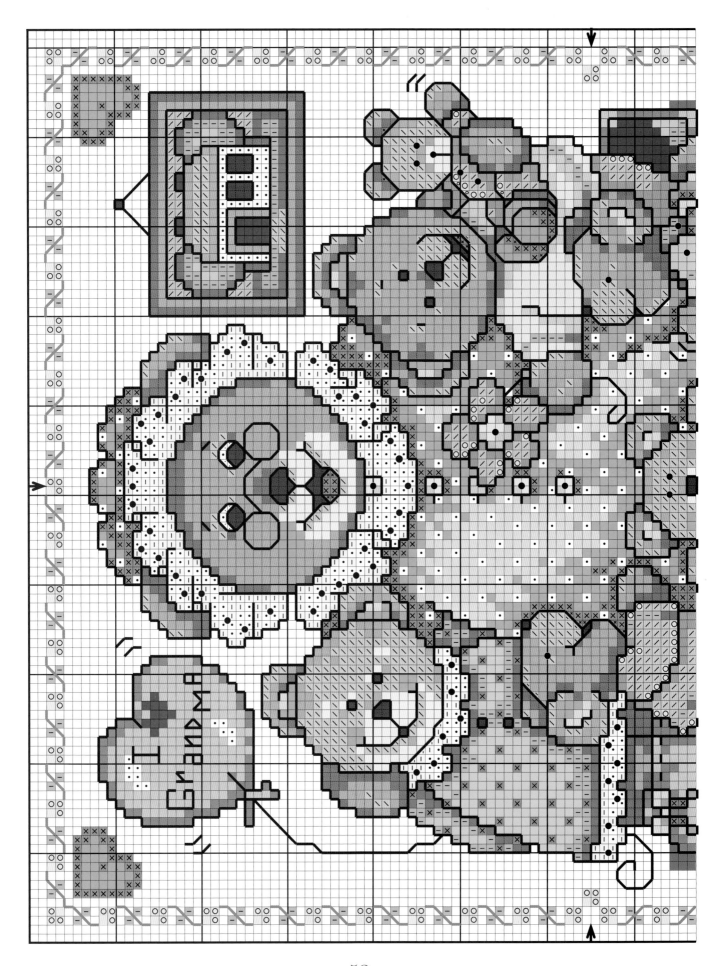

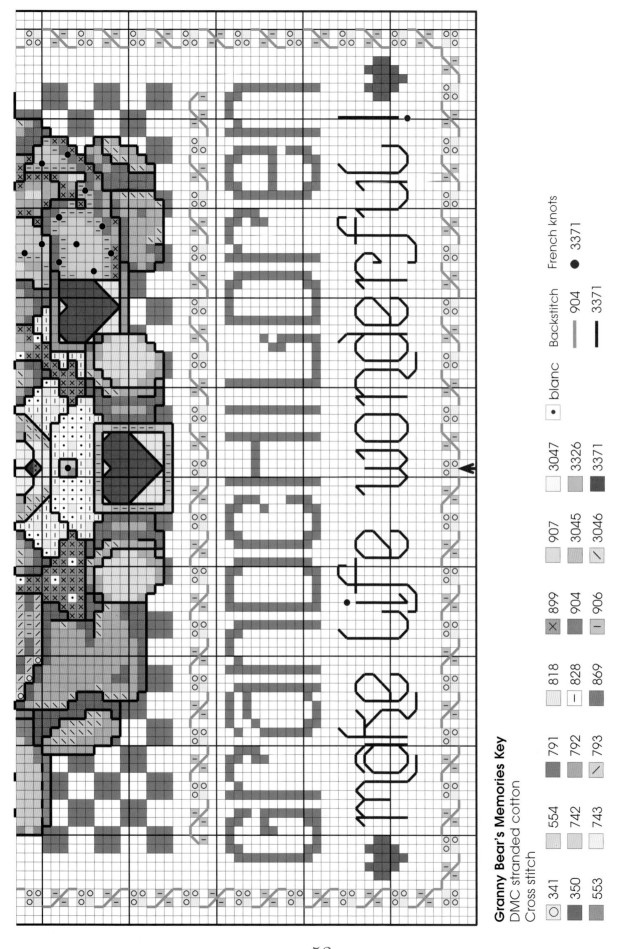

Granny Bear's Memories Key
DMC stranded cotton
Cross stitch

○ 341	791
350	792
553	╱ 793
554	818
742	— 828
743	869

✕ 899	907	3047
904	3045	3326
— 906	3046	3371

| • blanc |

Backstitch
— 904
— 3371

French knots
● 3371

Teddy Greetings

TEDDY BEARS EXPRESS their feelings with a glint in their eye and a tilt of their head and are perfect for all sorts of greetings cards, as this collection shows. Celebrate a wedding or anniversary with the loving teddy bear couple. Send best wishes from a little bear and smiling star. Wish good luck to a new home-owner with a home sweet home teddy. Say thank you with a bashful teddy and her tulip bouquet. Reward a job well done with a teddy holding a banner while confetti flies, and brighten the day for an ailing friend with a teddy bear nurse and her cheering bouquet of fresh-cut flowers.

Teddy Greetings

Design Sizes (each card)
6 x 8cm (2¼ x 3in)
Stitch Counts (each card)
42w x 57h

MATERIALS (for each card)
18 x 20cm (7 x 8in) Fiddler's
Light 18-count Aida

♥

DMC stranded cotton (floss)
as listed in chart key

♥

Tapestry needle number 24

1 Prepare for work, referring to Techniques. Find and mark the centre of the fabric and mount in an embroidery frame if you wish.

2 Start stitching from the centre of the chart, using two strands of stranded cotton (floss) for cross stitches and French knots (wound once around the needle). Backstitch all outlines using one strand of 310 (shown in grey on the charts for clarity).

3 Once all the stitching is complete, mount your embroidery in a suitable card (see page 108 and also suggestions on decorating card mounts).

Some tender words of kindness
Perhaps to say hello,
A Teddy Bear can tell you
All you need to know.

How wonderful to have one
Settled by my side,
To make our home a joyous place
Where faith and love abide.

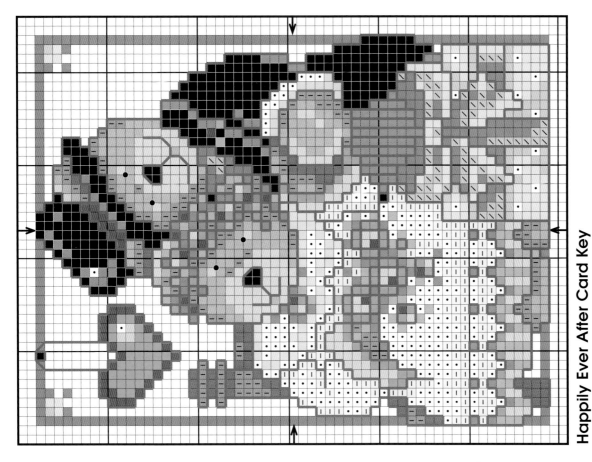

Happily Ever After Card Key

DMC stranded cotton
Cross stitch

▨ 309	▨ 470	▨ 729	╱ 3755
■ 310	▨ 471	⊟ 747	⊟ 3829
▨ 317	▨ 676	▨ 869	▨ 3841
▨ 334	▨ 725	▨ 899	・ blanc
▨ 415	▨ 726	▨ 3326	

Backstitch ▬▬ 310
French knots ● 310

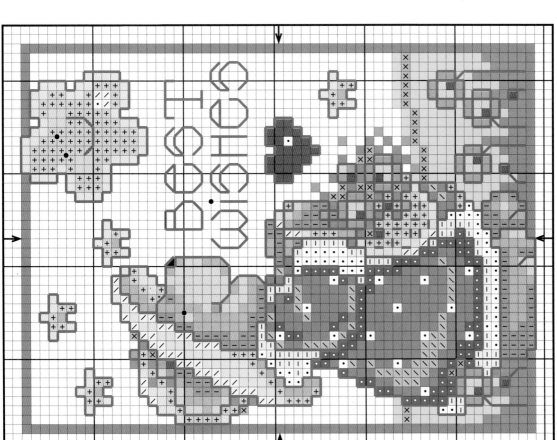

Best Wishes Card Key

DMC stranded cotton
Cross stitch

▨ 309	✕ 471	╱ 727	▨ 3326
■ 310	▨ 472	▨ 729	╱ 3755
▨ 312	▨ 676	⊟ 747	⊟ 3829
▨ 334	＋ 725	▨ 899	・ blanc
▨ 470	▨ 726	▨ 972	

Backstitch ▬▬ 310
French knots ● 310

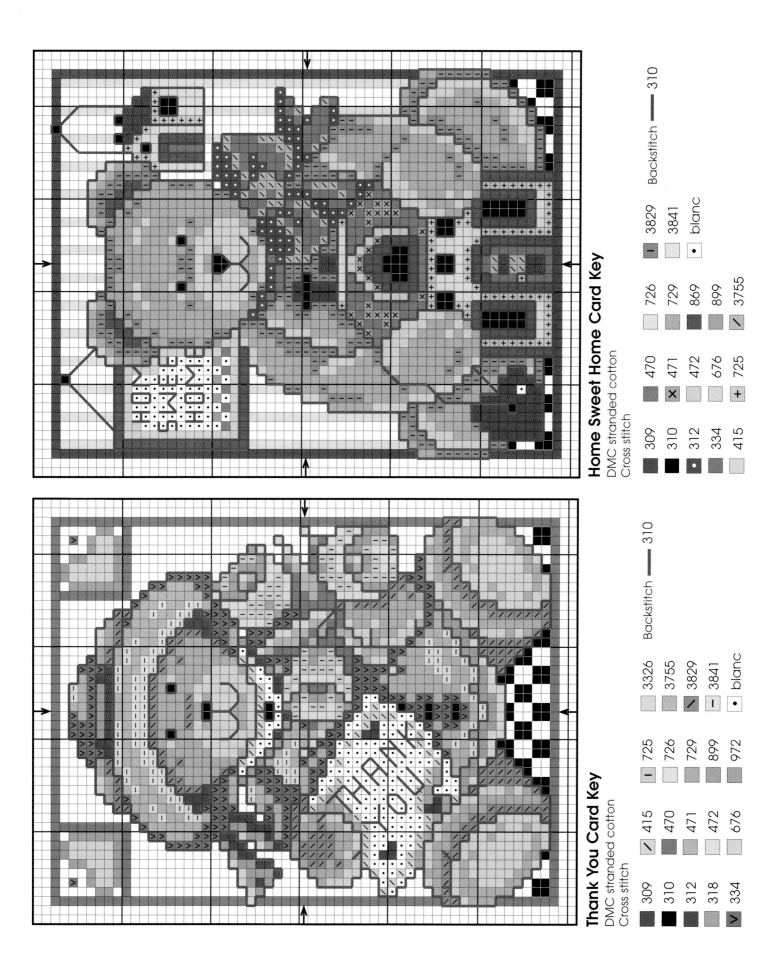

Home Sweet Home Card Key
DMC stranded cotton
Cross stitch

Backstitch ——— 310

309	470	726	3829
310	471 (×)	729	3841
312	472	869	blanc (•)
334	676	899	
415	725 (+)	3755 (/)	

Thank You Card Key
DMC stranded cotton
Cross stitch

Backstitch ——— 310

309	415 (/)	3326	725 (I)
310	470	3755	726
312	471	3829 (/)	729
318	472	3841	899
334 (>)	676	blanc (•)	972

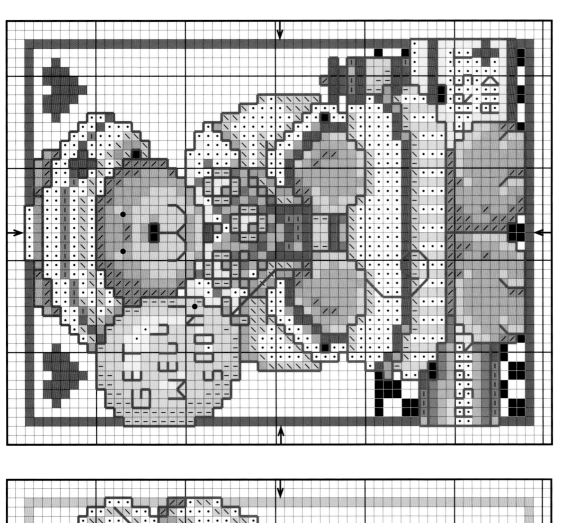

Get Well Soon Card Key

DMC stranded cotton
Cross stitch

▨ 309	▨ 415	▨ 725	▨ 869	▪ blanc
■ 310	▨ 470	▨ 726	▨ 899	
▨ 312	▨ 471	▨ 727	▨ 972	
▨ 318	▨ 472	▨ 729	▨ 3755	
▨ 334	▨ 676	▨ 747	╱ 3829	

Backstitch ——— 310
French knots ● 310

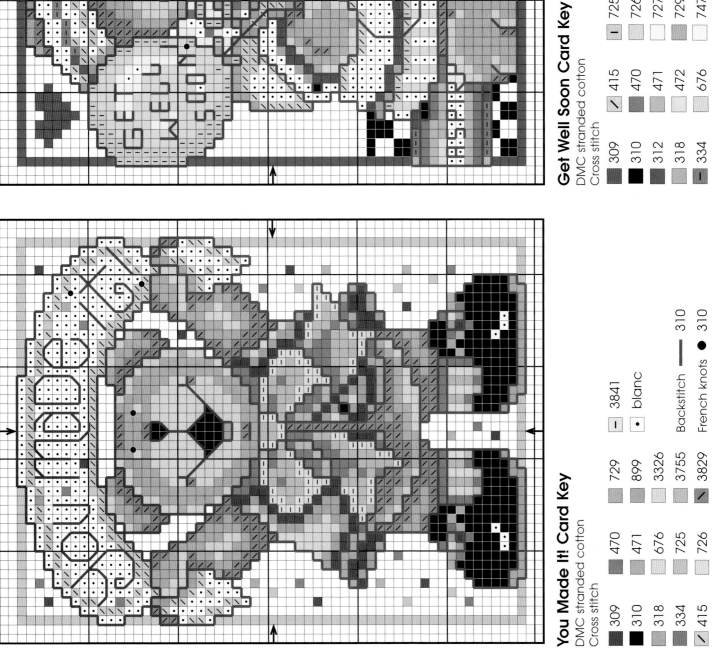

You Made It! Card Key

DMC stranded cotton
Cross stitch

▨ 309	▨ 470	▨ 729	▨ 3841	▪ blanc
■ 310	▨ 471	▨ 899		
▨ 318	▨ 676	▨ 3326		
▨ 334	▨ 725	▨ 3755		
╱ 415	▨ 726	╱ 3829		

Backstitch ——— 310
French knots ● 310

59

Birthday Bears

THERE'S A FESTIVE FEELING in the air and the bears are ready for a party! Gleefully they dance, calling us to join the fun and celebrate. These bears will add an extra touch of cheer to your birthday trimmings. A bright hanging banner of three dancing bears will show in all the honoured guests. Worked on 18-count Aida, each individual teddy can be easily made into a matching card. To complete the set, a colourful parade of teddy bear clowns dance with joy around an easily attached cake band.

Birthday Cake Band

Design Size
6.75cm (2⅝in) x circumference of cake plus turnings

Stitch Count
40h x circumference of cake

MATERIALS
8cm (3⅛in) wide 16-count white Aida band

♥

DMC stranded cotton (floss) as listed in chart key

♥

Tapestry needle number 24

♥

Adhesive tape

1 To calculate the length of Aida band required, measure the circumference of your cake tin (pan), adding 5cm (2in) for finishing the cut ends.

2 Begin stitching 5cm (2in) in from one short edge of the band, following the chart on pages 64 and 65 and repeating the band design as many times as necessary to fit your cake (the red dotted lines show the pattern repeat). Use two strands of stranded cotton (floss) for the cross stitches and the French knots (wrapped once around the needle) and one strand for all the backstitch outlines.

*Today will be a special day
Prepare for a surprise.
The Teddy Bears are
dancing 'round
And joy shines in their eyes.*

*I would not tell their secret
But the air is oh so gay.
Make way for celebration
On this very perfect day!*

3 Once the embroidery is complete, turn the ends of the band under by 1.25cm (½in) and stitch down. Wrap the band around the cake and fix with adhesive tape.

Birthday Banner

Design Size
(for each design)
7.5 x 10.5cm (3 x 4in)
Stitch Count
42w x 58h

MATERIALS
Three 20 x 23cm (8 x 9in)
pieces white 14-count Aida

♥

DMC stranded cotton (floss)
as listed in chart key

♥

Tapestry needle number 24

♥

0.5m (½yd) background fabric

♥

0.25m (¼yd) fusible fleece

♥

Three 0.5m (½yd) lengths of
decorative corded braid to
tone with embroideries

♥

Four large and three small
decorative buttons

♥

Matching sewing thread

♥

46cm (18in) length of 1.25cm
(½in) diameter dowel painted
to tone with embroidery

1 Find and mark the centres of the fabric pieces. Start stitching from the centre of the charts and the centres of the fabric, using two strands of stranded cotton (floss) for cross stitch and the French knots (wound once around the needle). Backstitch all outlines using one strand of 3371.

2 Once stitching is complete, make up as a banner as follows. Cut two 23 x 47cm (9 x 18½in) pieces of background fabric plus four 15 x 10cm (6 x 4in) pieces for tabs. Cut a piece of fusible fleece the same size as the background fabric. Fuse this to the wrong side of one of the fabric pieces, following manufacturer's instructions. Position the three embroideries on

Birthday Banner Key
DMC stranded cotton
Cross stitch

	334
	553
	554
	725
	742
	899
	906
	907
	3045
	3046
-	3047
	3325
	3326
	3371
•	blanc

Backstitch
— 3371

French knots
● 3371

the right side of the fleece-lined fabric (see diagram page 65), sewing or fusing them on according to the instructions on page 107. Stitch or glue a length of decorative braid around the edge of each embroidery, starting and ending at the centre bottom. To finish, sew a small decorative button on to each embroidery at centre bottom (see photograph).

3 To make the tabs, fold each piece of 15 x 10cm (6 x 4in) fabric in half lengthwise, right sides together. Sew a 1.25cm (½in) seam down the length and form a point at the end. Trim the seam, turn right side out and press. Now place the tabs evenly on the right side of the banner front with the points towards the centre. Pin in place, matching raw edges.

4 Place the second piece of background fabric on top with right sides together. Stitch a 1.25cm (½in) seam all around leaving a gap for turning. Turn right side out, press and slipstitch the gap closed. Bring the loose ends of the tabs to the front and sew on a large decorative button at each point. Insert the dowel through the tabs, ready to hang the banner.

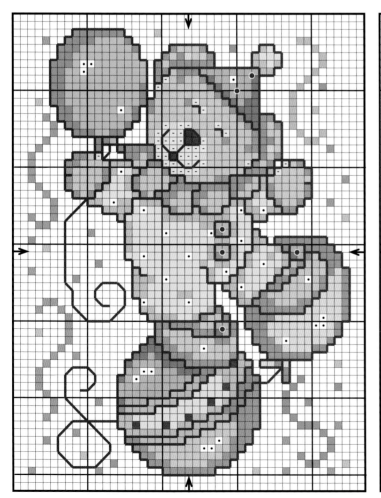

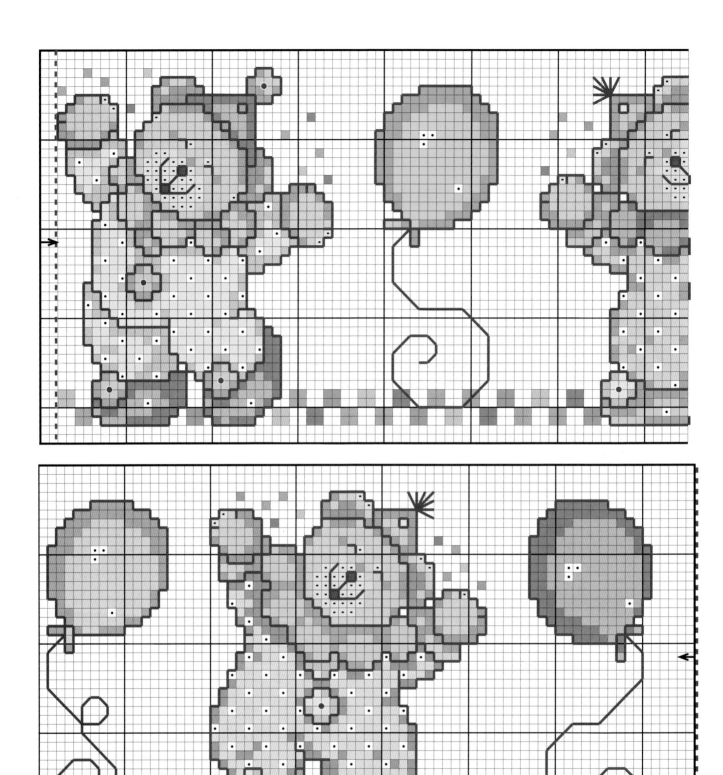

Cake Band Key

DMC stranded cotton
Cross stitch

	334		725		906		3046		3326	Backstitch —— 3371
	553		742		907	-	3047		3371	French knots ● 3371
	554		899		3045		3325	●	blanc	Pattern repeat - - - -

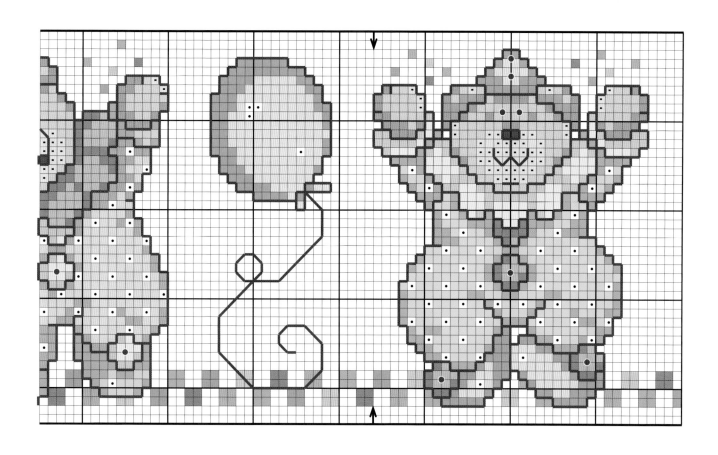

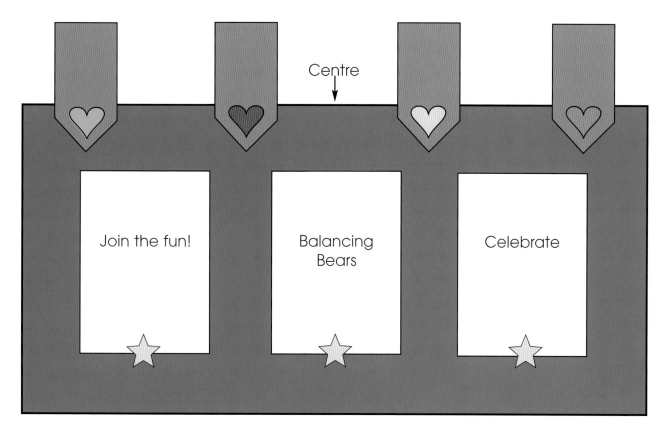

Centre

Join the fun!

Balancing
Bears

Celebrate

True Friends Teddies

THERE IS LITTLE IN THIS WORLD MORE dear than the gift of a true friend. Through all the sorrows and joys that life can contain, they remain a constant source of comfort and sharing, never failing. A friend offers gentle consolation, sound advice and genuine love. In this picture, two little true friend teddies walk hand-in-hand, sharing confidences on a day filled with the sweet scent of the flowers at their feet. Surrounded by tender pink hearts, they speak of all the blessings a treasured friend can bring.

Design Size
18.5 x 23cm (7¼ x 9in)
Stitch Count
101w x 126h

MATERIALS
30 x 36cm (12 x 14in) antique white 14-count Aida
♥
DMC stranded cotton (floss) as listed in chart key
♥
Tapestry needle number 24

1 Prepare for work, referring to Techniques. Find and mark the centre of the fabric and mount in a frame if you wish.

2 Start stitching from the centre of the chart and fabric, working all cross stitches using two strands of stranded cotton (floss) and the French knots on the noses with two strands of white wound once around the needle. Work the French knots in the flower centres using two strands of 3345 wound once around the needle. Work the backstitch flower stems using one strand of 3345. Use one strand of

310 to outline eyes, noses and mouths and one strand of 938 for all other backstitch outlines.

3 Once stitching is complete, finish your picture by mounting and framing (see page 108).

Dearest Teddy, sweet as Spring
Such warmth and comfort
you do bring.
You're always there
to be my friend
Ever faithful, to the end.

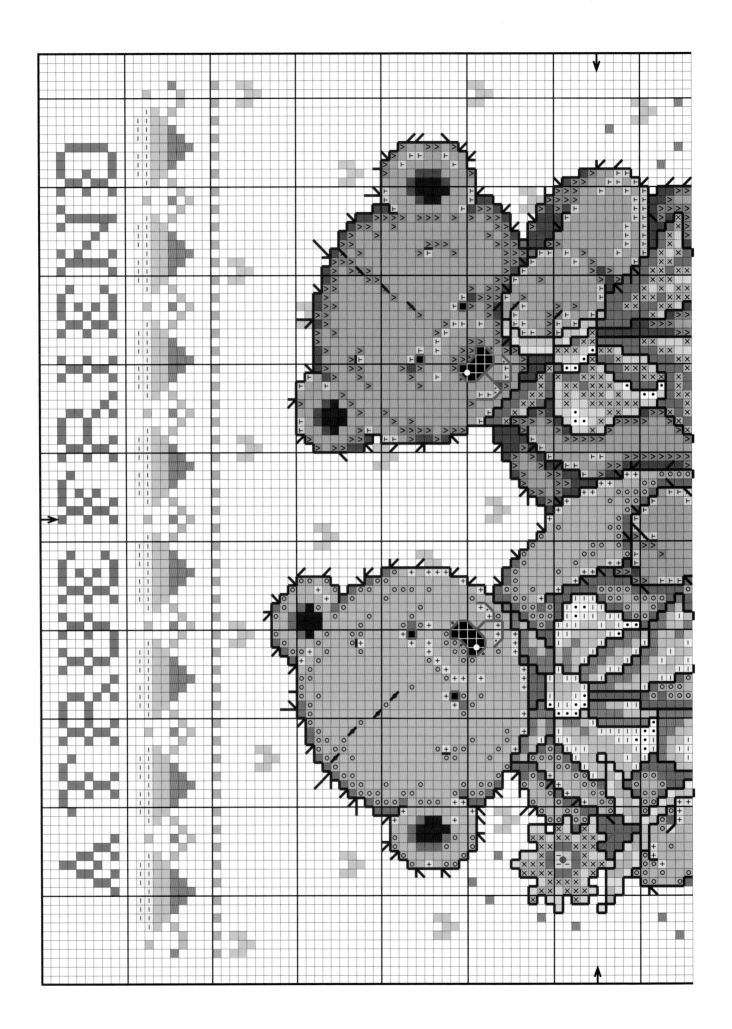

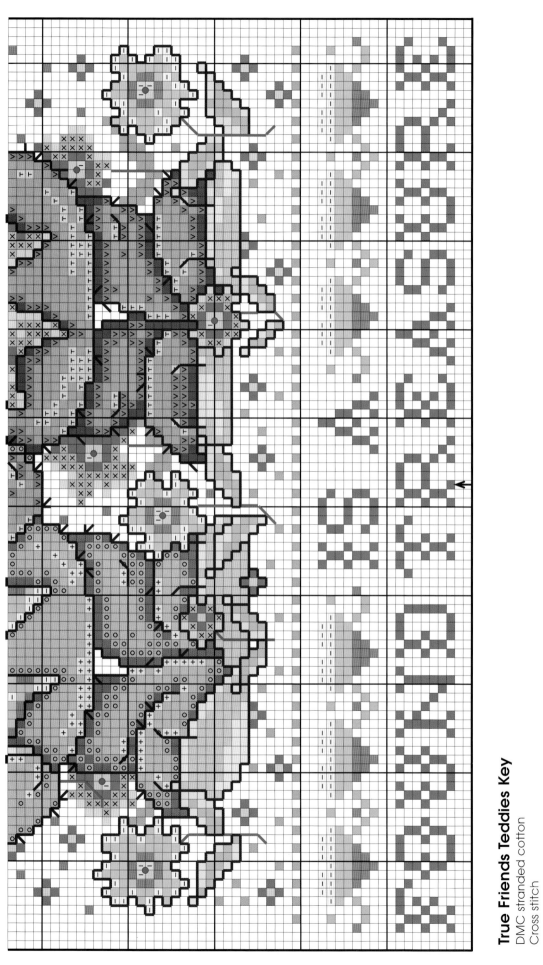

True Friends Teddies Key

DMC stranded cotton
Cross stitch

	310		435
	368		436
○	420	⊤	437
	433		471

	472		3045		3689		3838
	869	+	3046		3773	✕	3839
	938		3687		3820		3840
	950		3688	⊤	3822	•	blanc

Backstitch
—— 310
—— 938
—— 3345

French knots
● 3345
○ blanc

Flower Seed Teddy

A GARDEN IS A SPECIAL PLACE, a bit of heaven on earth where we can create a palette of colours and scents pleasing to the eye and intoxicating to the senses. Inside the potting shed, amongst the tools and seeds, sits a gardening teddy. Busy at work, she has planted a pot of colourful poppies to bring the consolation of rest after a hard day's work. This framed picture will bring the pleasures of the gardener's world inside for all to enjoy.

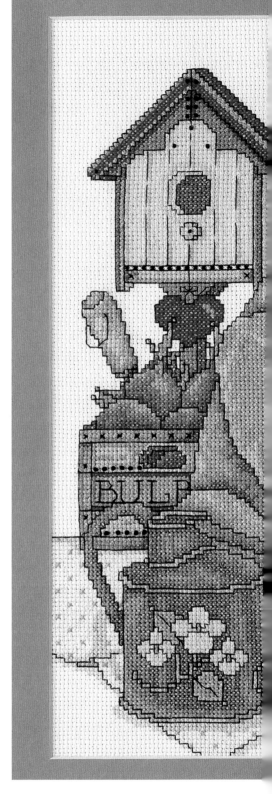

Design Size
41 x 29cm (16 x 11½in)
Stitch Count
223w x 161h

MATERIALS
53 x 40cm (21 x 16in) white
14-count Aida

♥

DMC stranded cotton (floss)
as listed in chart key

♥

Tapestry needle number 24

1 Prepare fabric for work, referring to Techniques. Find and mark the centre of the fabric and mount in a frame if you wish.

2 Start stitching from the centre of the chart and fabric, working all cross stitches using two strands of stranded cotton (floss). Some colours use more than one skein. Work the French knots in the eyes with two strands of white wound once around the needle and all other French knots using black 310. Work all backstitches using one strand of 310.

3 Once you have finished all the stitching, check the embroidery is complete and then finish your picture by mounting and framing (see page 108 for guidance).

Sitting in my garden
Beneath the summer sky,
Taking in the beauty
What do I espy?

The softest sense of movement
Amongst the flowers fair.
It's really quite a lovely thing
A gardening Teddy Bear!

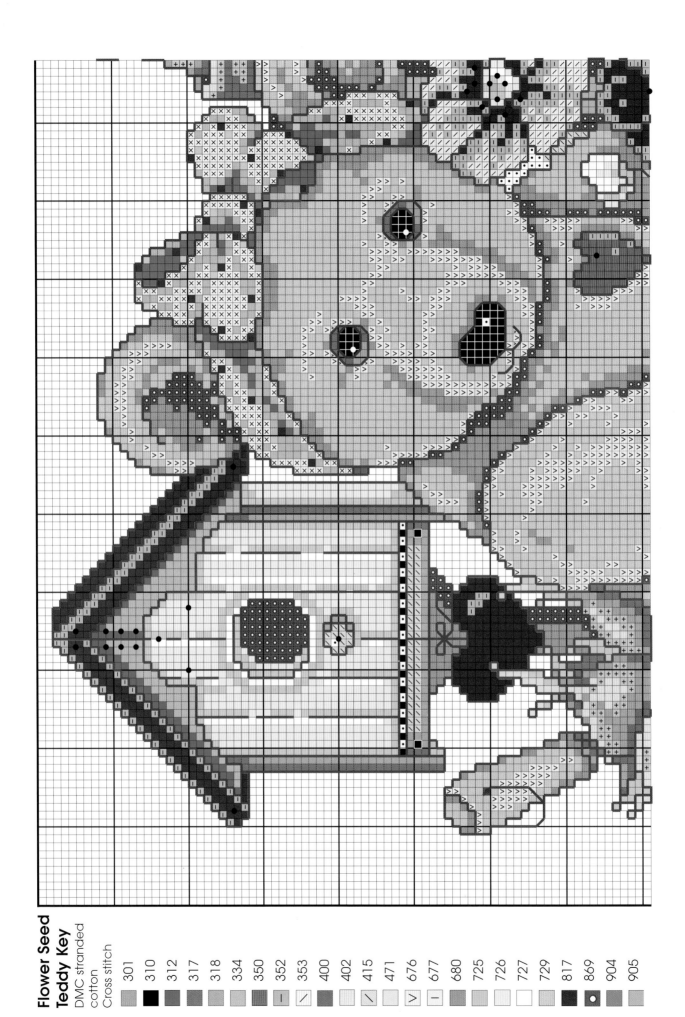

**Flower Seed
Teddy Key**

DMC stranded
cotton
Cross stitch

| 301 | 310 | 312 | 317 | 318 | 334 | 350 | 352 | 353 | 400 | 402 | 415 | 471 | 676 | 677 | 680 | 725 | 726 | 727 | 729 | 817 | 869 | 904 | 905 |

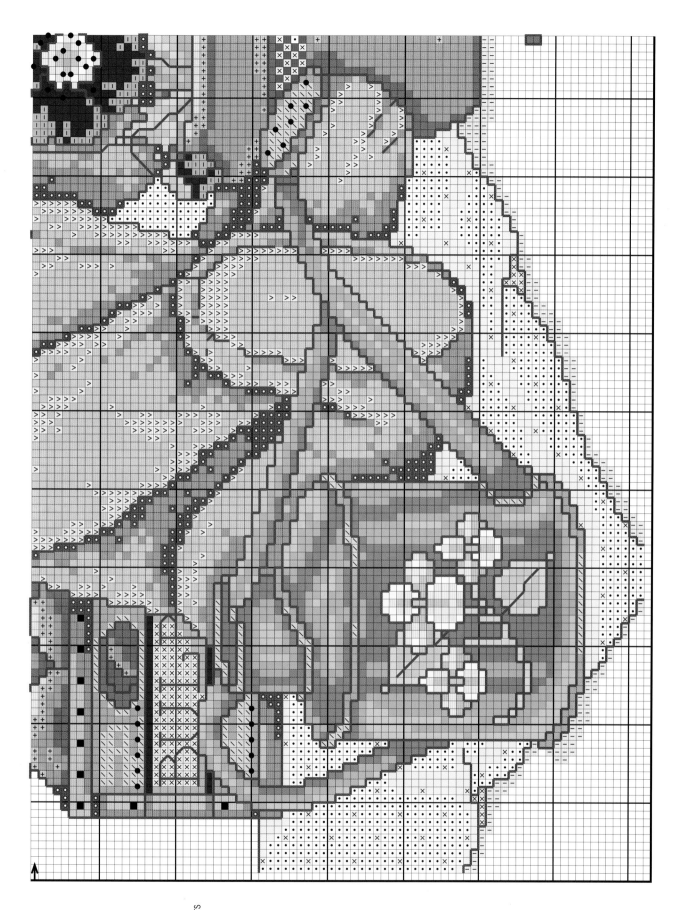

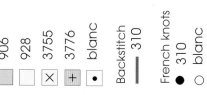

906
928
3755
3776
blanc

Backstitch
—— 310

French knots
● 310
○ blanc

73

| DMC stranded cotton Cross stitch | 301 | 310 | 312 | 317 | 318 | 334 | 350 | 352 | 353 | 400 | 402 | 415 | 471 | 676 | 677 | 680 | 725 | 726 | 727 | 729 | 817 | 869 | 904 | 905 |

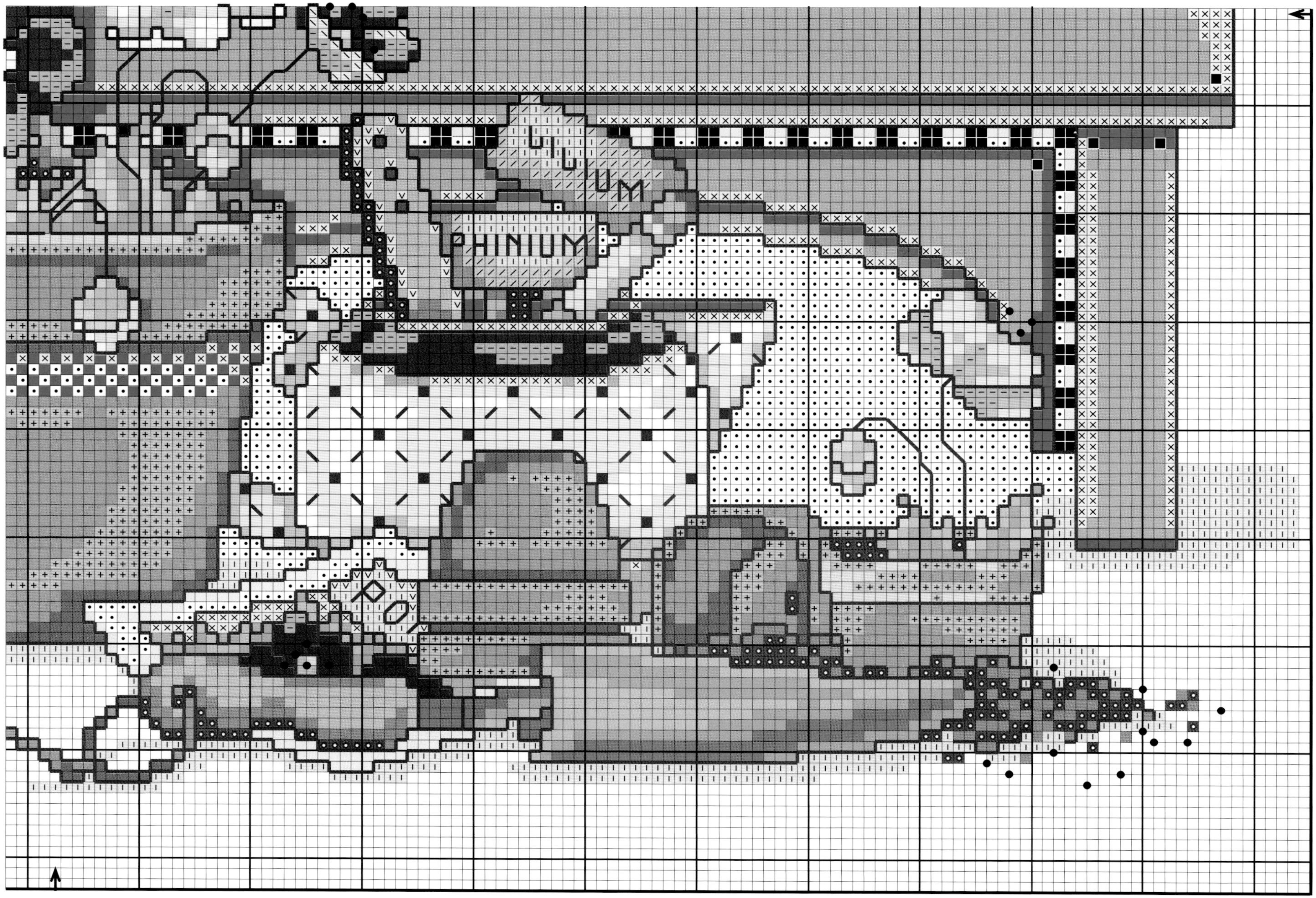

906
928
× 3755
+ 3776
• blanc

Backstitch
310

French knots
● 310
○ blanc

Teddy Bear Guests

THE WELCOMING ARMS of a teddy take us to a sweet world of comfort and ease. They bid us to relax and leave the cares of the day behind. Place this teddy guest set out for your overnight visitors and it is sure to bring a smile. The checkered borders and country colours will lend a cosy feel to your guest room. Matching his and her towels and a wooden hand mirror will help weary travellers freshen up after their journey and a delightful wooden trinket bowl holds jewellery or other treasures.

Hand Mirror

Design Sizes
Mirror: 11 x 11cm (4¼ x 4¼in)
on 14-count
Trinket Bowl: 8.5 x 8.5cm
(3¼ x 3¼in) on 18-count

Stitch Counts
Mirror: 61w x 61h
Trinket Bowl: 61w x 61h

MATERIALS
20 x 20cm (8 x 8in) Rustico
14-count Aida (Zweigart #54)

♥

DMC stranded cotton (floss)
as listed in chart key

♥

Tapestry needle number 24

♥

46cm (18in) decorative
braided cord

♥

Large hand mirror (Sudberry
House #23301 – see Suppliers)

♥

Permanent fabric glue

♥

One decorative bow

1 Prepare for work, referring to Techniques if necessary. Find and mark the centre of the fabric and mount in an embroidery frame if you wish.

2 Start stitching from the centre of the chart and fabric, using two strands of stranded cotton (floss) for cross stitches and French knots (wound once around the needle). Work backstitch outlines using one strand according to the colours on the chart. (Note: the trinket bowl uses the same chart and key but is stitched on a smaller count fabric to make a smaller embroidery.)

3 Once the embroidery is complete, mount it in the hand mirror following the manufacturer's instructions. Attach the decorative cording with a thin bead of fabric glue all around the edge of the mounted embroidery, starting at centre bottom. Press the cording in place, then glue on a decorative bow to hide the cut ends of the cord.

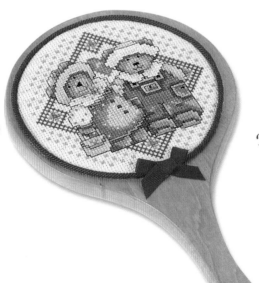

*A hale and hearty welcome
To all who enter here.
May peace be ever with you
Should you be far or near.*

*The Teddy Bears will greet you
And do this message send:
Our house is always open
To you our precious friends.*

Hand Mirror and Trinket Bowl Key

DMC stranded cotton
Cross stitch

• blanc	╱ 470	869	▮ 3688	Backstitch	French knots
■ 310	471	972	3689	── 310	● 310
312	725	3045	3755	── 469	● 3687
322	− 726	3046			○ blanc
415	╲ 762	3687			

79

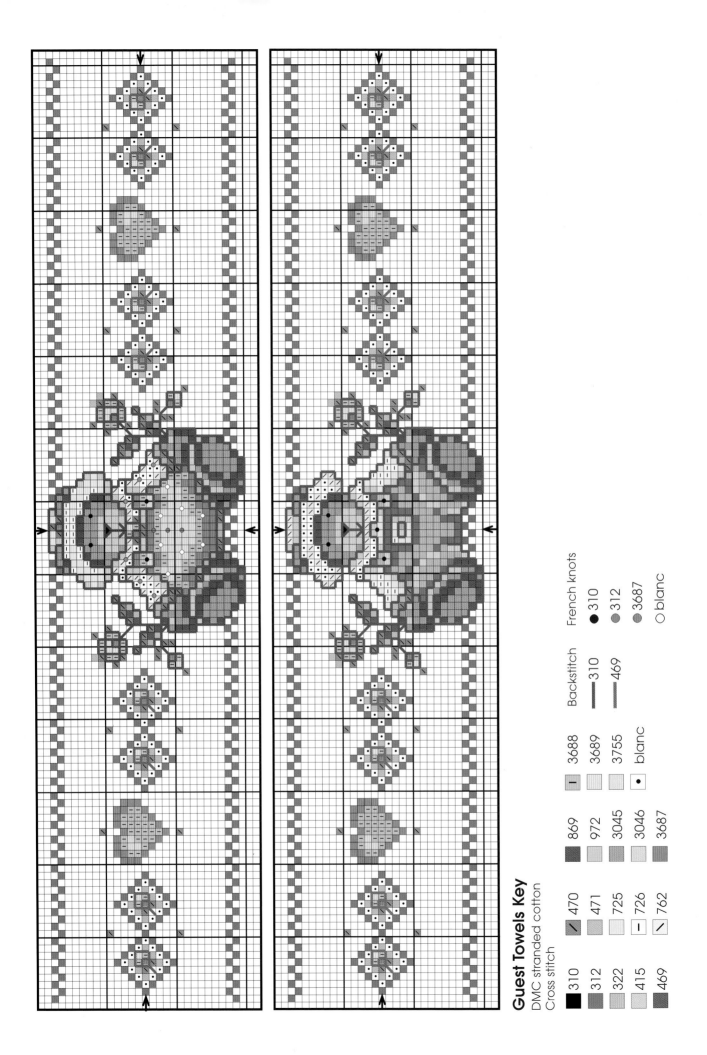

Guest Towels Key

DMC stranded cotton
Cross stitch

■ 310	▨ 470	▨ 869	▬ 3688		Backstitch
▨ 312	▨ 471	▨ 972	▨ 3689		—— 310
▨ 322	▨ 725	▨ 3045	▨ 3755		—— 469
▨ 415	– 726	▨ 3046	• blanc		
▨ 469	╲ 762	▨ 3687			French knots
					● 310
					● 312
					● 3687
					○ blanc

Guest Towels

Design Size (for each towel)
24 x 5cm (9½ x 2in)
Stitch Counts
130w x 28h

MATERIALS

Guest towel with 14-count
ecru insert (Charles Craft
#6682-2724 – see Suppliers)

♥

DMC stranded cotton (floss)
as listed in chart key

♥

Tapestry needle number 24

1   Find the centre
of the embroidery
insert on the towel
and begin stitching
the border from here outwards.

2 Following the chart (left), use
two strands of stranded cotton
(floss) for the cross stitches and the
French knots (wrapped once
around the needle). Work all the
backstitch outlines using one
strand.

3 Once all stitching is complete,
press the towel from the back.

Trinket Bowl

Design Size
8.5 x 8.5cm (3⅜ x 3⅜in)
Stitch Count
61w x 61h

MATERIALS

20 x 20cm (8 x 8in) Rustico
18-count Aida (Zweigart #54)

♥

DMC stranded cotton (floss)
as listed in chart key

♥

Tapestry needle number 24

♥

Wooden trinket bowl
(Framecraft #W4E – see
Suppliers)

1 Prepare for work,
referring to page 105
of the Techniques
section if necessary,
finding and marking the centre of
the fabric.

2 Following the chart on page
79, start stitching from the centre
of the chart and fabric, using two
strands of stranded cotton (floss)
for the cross stitches and French
knots (wrapped once around the
needle). Work the backstitch outlines using one strand.

3 Once stitching is complete,
mount in the bowl lid, according
to the manufacturer's instructions.

If You Sprinkle. . .

WASHING, CLEANING, COOKING, SHOPPING. . . it always seems that a mother's work is never done. In this picture, a whimsical Mama bear, dressed in a crisp white apron and fluffy green house slippers, is busy tending to her chores. The border of tiny blue and pink flowers brings a fresh touch of the countryside to the smallest room in the house. Stitch up this gentle reminder to bring a smile to their faces while gently coaxing the whole family to do their part.

Design Size
18 x 23cm (7 x 9in)
Stitch Count
100w x 128h

MATERIALS
30 x 35cm (12 x 14in) white
14-count Aida

♥

DMC stranded cotton (floss)
as listed in chart key

♥

Tapestry needle number 24

1 Prepare for work, referring to Techniques. Find and mark the centre of the fabric and mount in a frame if you wish.

2 Start stitching from the centre of the chart and fabric, using two strands of stranded cotton (floss) for cross stitches and French knots (wound once around the needle). Work the various backstitches using one strand.

3 Once stitching is complete, finish your picture by mounting and framing (see page 108).

*When washing day
comes around
The Teddies run and hide.
They try to miss their
bath time
And the hanging out to dry.
But mother bear is ready,
She's waiting on the path
To scoop them in her apron
And send them to the bath.*

If you sprinkle
when you tinkle...

be a sweetie...
and wipe the seatie.

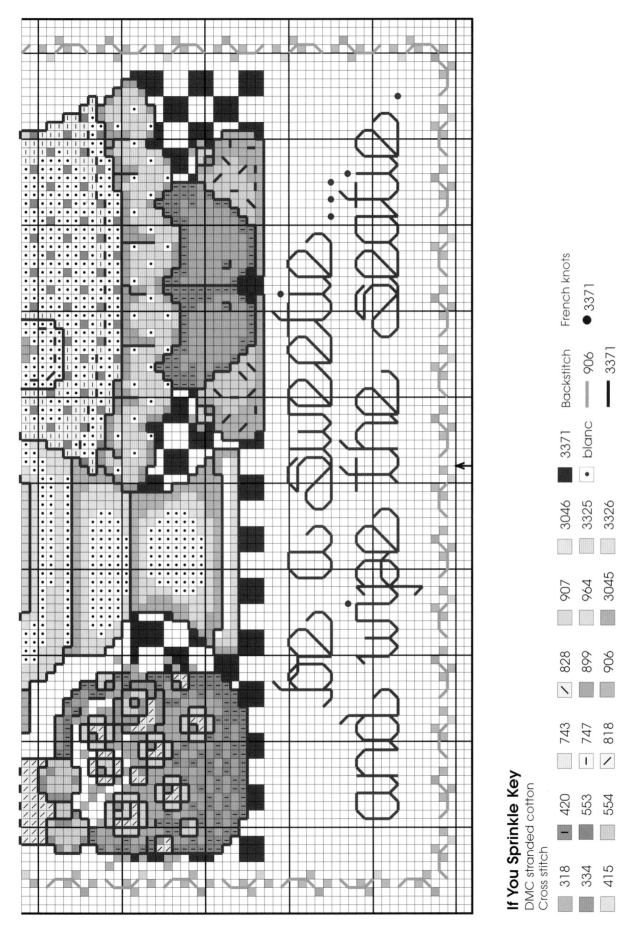

If You Sprinkle Key

DMC stranded cotton

Cross stitch

318	420	743	828
334	553	747	899
415	554	818	906

907	3046	3371
964	3325	
3045	3326	

Backstitch
— 906
— 3371

French knots
● 3371

Alphabet Bears

B is most definitely for bears! Whether they are busy gardening, sending a letter, serving tea, or just saying I love you, these alphabet bears invite everyone into their colourful world. Create the large sampler to display in a child's room or for yourself. Combine individual letters for other projects. A sachet or trinket box would make a darling hostess gift or token of thanks. Make up a name plate for a room or office, or use your imagination and combine the letters on your own creations.

Alphabet Bears Sampler

Design Size
32 x 41.5cm (12¾ x 16¼in)
Stitch Count
203w x 262h

MATERIALS
43 x 53cm (17 x 21in) Fiddler's Light 16-count Aida (Charles Craft)
♥
DMC stranded cotton (floss) as listed in chart key
♥
Tapestry needle number 24

1 Prepare for work, referring to Techniques. Mark the centre of the fabric and mount in a frame. It would help to enlarge the chart on a colour photocopier.

2 Start stitching from the centre of the fabric and chart (on pages 88–93), using two strands of stranded cotton (floss) for cross stitches and French knots (wound once around the needle). Work the variously coloured backstitches with one strand. The blue letters are outlined in 336.

3 Once stitching is complete, finish your picture by mounting and framing (see page 108).

A is for Apple,
B is for Bear,
C is for Caring
like my Teddy Bear
D is for Day-time,
E is for Eve,
F is Forever, so Teddies believe.

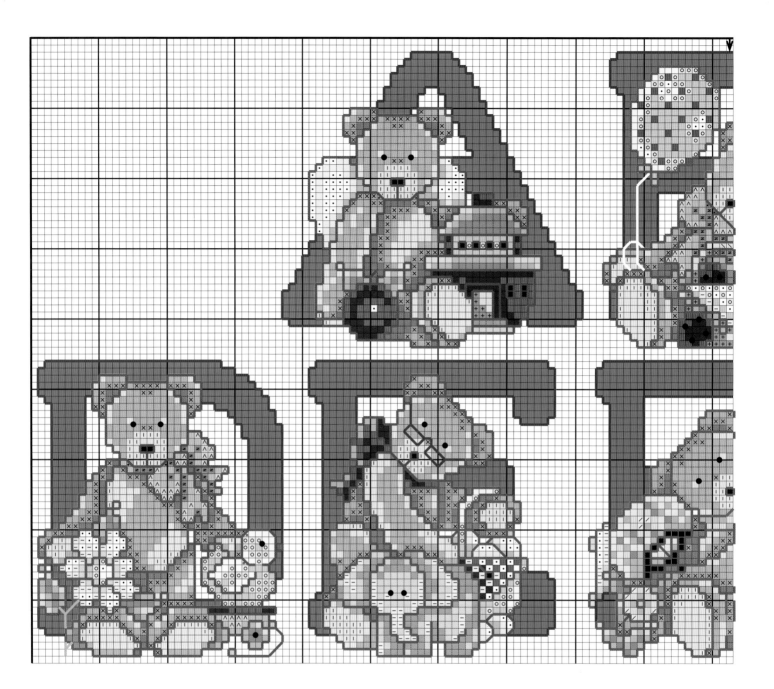

MATERIALS

20 x 20cm (8 x 8in) Fiddler's
Light 18-count Aida (Charles
Craft)

♥

DMC stranded cotton (floss)
as listed in chart key

♥

Tapestry needle number 24

♥

Wooden trinket bowl
(Framecraft #W4R – see
Suppliers)

Trinket Bowl Lid

1 Choose your letter – see the main chart for individual letters' stitch counts (calculate design size by dividing stitch count by fabric count). Prepare for work, marking the centre of the fabric. Start stitching from the centre, using two strands of stranded cotton (floss) for cross stitches and French knots (wound once around the needle) and one strand for backstitches.

2 Once all the stitching is complete, mount your embroidery in a trinket bowl lid following the manufacturer's instructions.

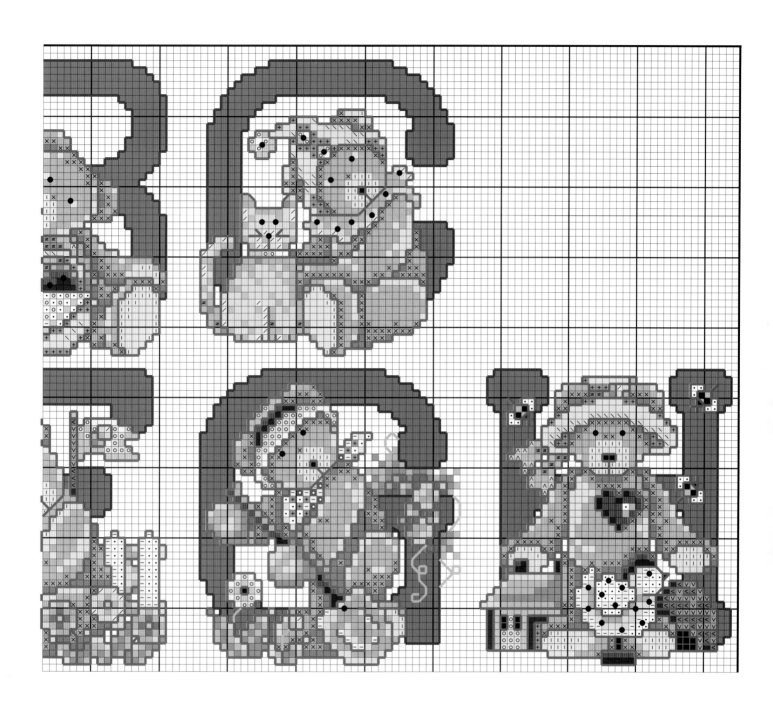

Alphabet Bears Sampler Key

DMC stranded cotton
Cross stitch

▨	208	⋏	341	Ι	677	⁄	818	•	blanc	**Backstitch**
▨	209	▨	350		725	▨	869			── 310
▨	211		415	○	726	▨	899		**French knots**	── 336
■	310	<	434		727	▨	964	•	208	── 471
▨	312	V	436		729	▨	3326	●	310	⋯⋯ 725
▨	318	▨	470		747	⊠	3746	●	350	── 817
◉	322	▨	471	−	762	▨	3755	●	725	══ blanc
+	334	▨	472	▨	801	✕	3829			
▨	340	▨	676	■	817	⟍	3841			

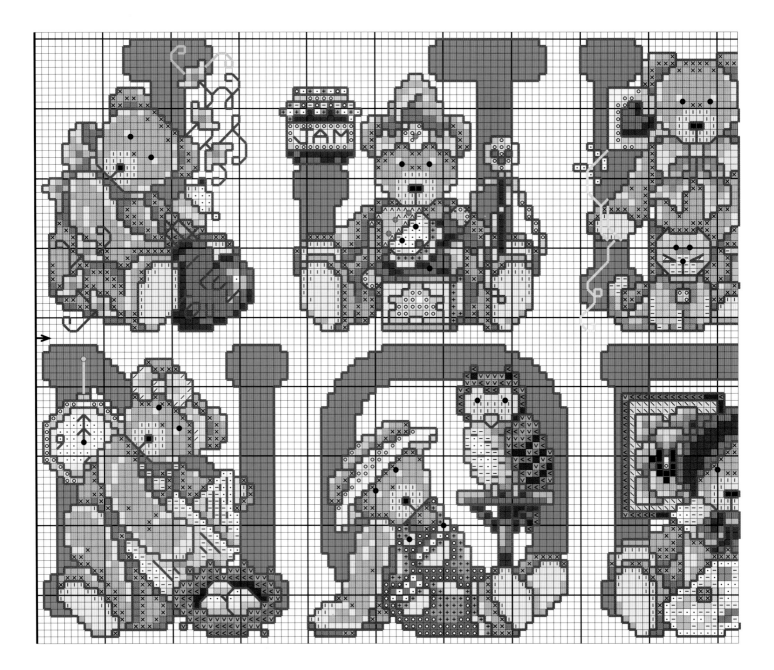

MATERIALS

20 x 20cm (8 x 8in) Fiddler's Light 14-count Aida (Charles Craft)

♥

DMC stranded cotton (floss) as listed in chart key

♥

Tapestry needle number 24

♥

Iron-on interfacing

♥

20 x 20cm (8 x 8in) backing fabric

46cm (18in) decorative cord or piping to tone with embroidery

♥

Polyester filling

♥

30cm (12in) ribbon (⅜in) to tone with embroidery

♥

One decorative bow to match ribbon

♥

Matching sewing thread

Sachet

1 Follow step 1 of the Trinket Bowl Lid on page 88 for preparation and stitching.

2 Once the embroidery is complete, make up into a sachet. Trim the embroidery leaving twelve rows beyond the edge all around. Cut a piece of iron-on interfacing to the same size and press on to the wrong side of the embroidery.

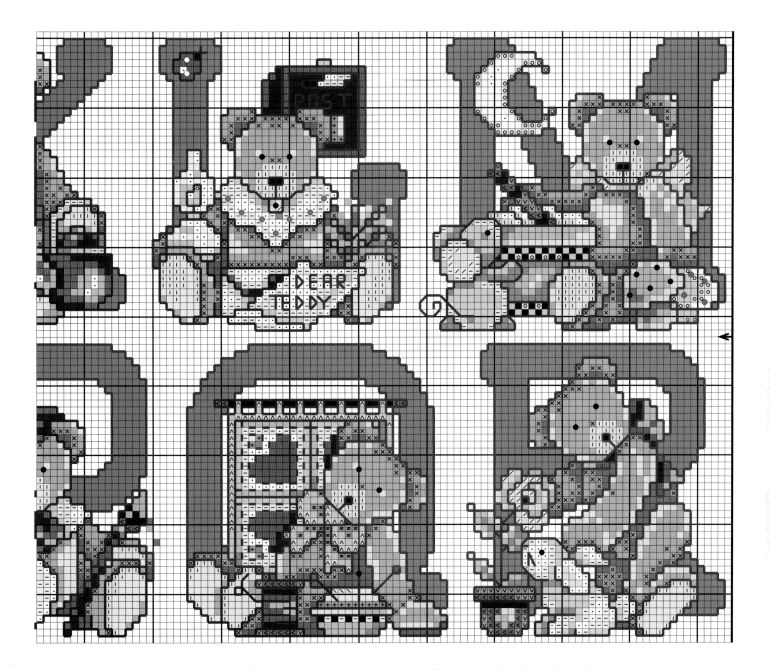

3 If using piping, tack (baste) it to the right side, six rows from the embroidery with raw edges matching, starting and ending at centre bottom.

4 To make the hanging loop, fold the ribbon in half lengthways and pin it to the right side of the front, with the loop pointing towards the centre. Now cut the backing fabric to the same size as the →

Alphabet Bears Sampler Key

DMC stranded cotton
Cross stitch

▨	208	∧	341	▐	677	╱	818	•	blanc
▨	209	▨	350	▨	725	▨	869		
▨	211	▨	415	O	726	▨	899		
■	310	<	434	▨	727	▨	964		
▨	312	V	436	▨	729	▨	3326		
▨	318	▨	470	▨	747	z	3746		
◉	322	▨	471	−	762	▨	3755		
+	334	▨	472	■	801	✕	3829		
▨	340	▨	676	▨	817	＼	3841		

French knots
- 208
- 310
- 350
- 725

Backstitch
— 310
— 336
— 471
— 725
— 817
— blanc

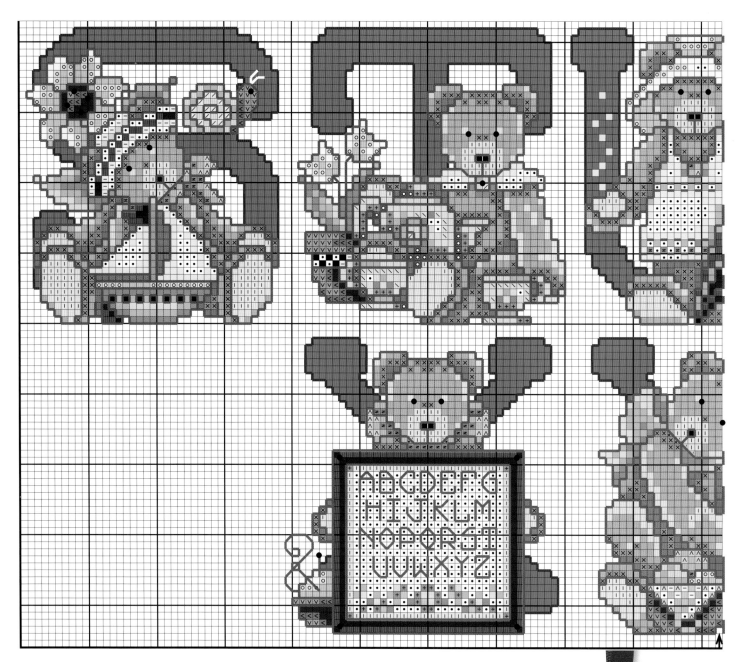

trimmed embroidery and pin in place, right sides facing. Stitch a 1.25cm (½in) seam all around, securing the hanging loop as you go, and leaving an opening for turning at the bottom edge. Turn through to right side and stuff with polyester filling.

5 If using decorative cord to trim the sachet, attach by slipstitching it around all edges, beginning and ending at centre bottom. Tuck the cord in at the bottom opening and slipstitch closed. To finish off, attach a decorative bow at the centre bottom of the sachet.

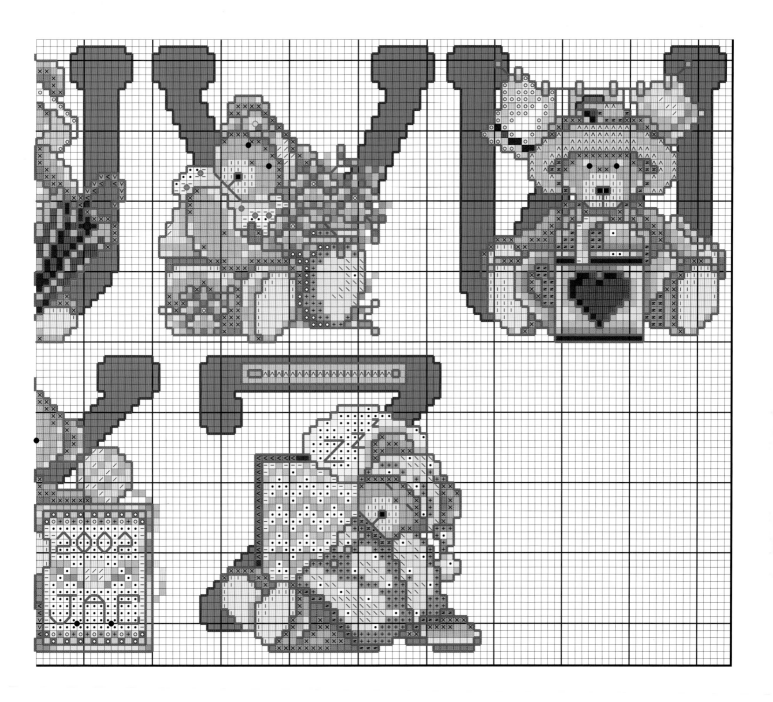

Alphabet Bears Sampler Key

DMC stranded cotton
Cross stitch

	208	∧	341	I	677	/	818	•	blanc	Backstitch	
	209		350		725		869			—	310
	211		415	O	726		899	French knots		—	336
	310	<	434		727		964	●	208	—	471
	312	V	436		729	z	3746	●	310	⋯⋯	725
	318		470		747		3755	●	350	—	817
O	322		471	−	762		3826	●	725	⟶	blanc
+	334		472		801	×	3829				
	340		676		817	\	3841				

Beary Merry Christmas

YOU CAN CAPTURE some of teddy's special charm with these adorable Christmas ornaments. Three angel bears ready to take flight are dressed in bright coats and scarves, their wings edged in gold metallic thread to add a shimmering touch. Three more bears are here too – one wishing you happy holidays, one peeking through a cheerful Christmas wreath and the last bringing a huge candy cane to share. Hang these whimsical friends from your tree with golden cord and enjoy!

MATERIALS

(for six ornaments)

One 20 x 28cm (8 x 11in) sheet white 14-count plastic canvas

♥

DMC stranded cotton (floss) as listed in chart key

♥

Tapestry needle number 24

♥

DMC metallic pearl thread 5282 for hanging

♥

20 x 28cm (8 x 11in) iron-on interfacing or felt for backing

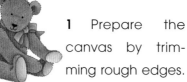

1 Prepare the canvas by trimming rough edges. You can stitch all the ornaments on one sheet of plastic canvas if you allow at least two bars between designs. Stitch counts and design sizes are with charts.

2 Using two strands of stranded cotton (floss), work cross stitches and French knots (wound once around the needle). Work all backstitches using one strand of 310.

3 After stitching is complete, back the ornaments with an iron-on interfacing such as Vilene or glue on pieces of felt, staying within the edges of the embroidery. Carefully cut out each orna-ment leaving one row of plastic canvas around the designs. At the top centre of each ornament thread a 30cm (12in) length of metallic pearl thread between the plastic edge and the stitching. Tie the ends in a secure bow to create a hanging loop.

Beneath the tree on
Christmas morn
A splendid sight I see,
All wrapped in ribbon,
paper and bows,
A teddy bear for me!

Angel Bear with Bauble

Design Size: 9.5 x 9cm (3¾ x 3½in)
Stitch Count: 53w x 48h

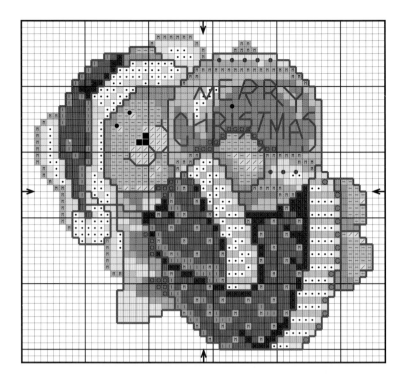

Angel Bear with Bell

Design Size: 10 x 9.75cm (4 x 3⅞in)
Stitch Count: 55w x 53h

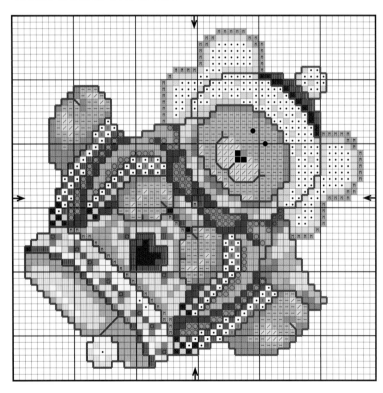

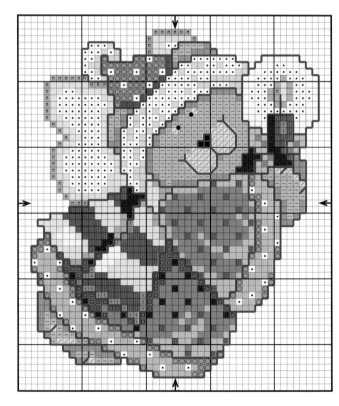

Angel Bear with Candle

Design Size: 8.25 x 9.75cm (3¼ x 3¾in)
Stitch Count: 45w x 53h

Christmas Bear in Wreath
Design Size: 5.5 x 4.75cm (2⅛ x 1⅞in)
Stitch Count: 30w x 26h

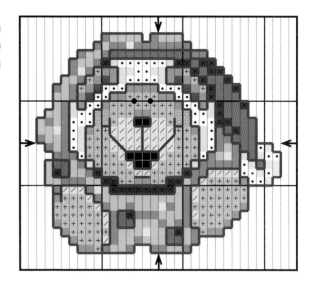

Christmas Bear with Candy Cane
Design Size: 5 x 7cm (2 x 2¾in)
Stitch Count: 27w x 39h

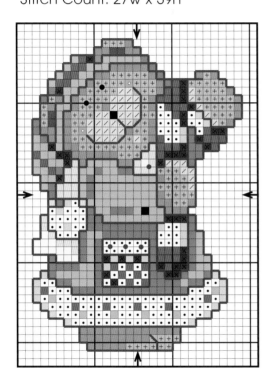

Beary Merry Christmas Key
DMC stranded cotton
Cross stitch

✕ 304	▎ 351	704	▉ 801	**Backstitch**	
☐ 307	– 676	725	○ 894	▬ 310	
■ 310	╱ 677	+ 729	3325	**French knots**	
▨ 312	680	742	M 5282	• 304	
○ 322	◻ 700	747	• blanc	● 310	
350	702	762			

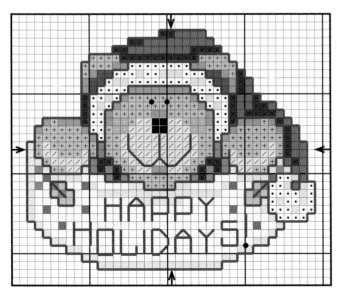

Christmas Bear Happy Holidays
Design Size: 6.75 x 5.5cm (2⅝ x 2⅛in)
Stitch Count: 37w x 30h

A Victorian Christmas

RICH RED AND GREEN satin ribbons, sparkling glass baubles, a Santa and snowman to hang on the tree, and of course a teddy bear. All these things make for a perfect, old-fashioned Christmas. This lovable honey-coloured bear sits amongst the treasures of Christmas past. Dressed in a red satin ruff, a holiday vest and his own Santa hat, he waits for his Christmas morning hug. Bring vintage charm to the holidays for yourself or someone dear with this wonderful stocking which has plenty of room for special treats for child and adult alike.

Design Size
25 x 38cm (10 x 15½in)
Stitch Count
139w x 219h

MATERIALS
38 x 50cm (15 x 20in) natural
14-count Aida

♥

DMC stranded cotton (floss)
as listed in chart key

♥

Tapestry needle number 24

♥

30 x 46cm (12 x 18in) fusible
fleece

♥

0.5m (½yd) backing and lining
fabric to tone with stocking

♥

150cm (60in) decorative braid
to tone with stocking

1 Prepare for work, referring to Techniques. Mark the centre of the fabric and mount in a frame. It would help to enlarge the chart on a colour photocopier.

2 Start stitching from the centre of the chart and fabric, using two strands of stranded cotton (floss) for cross stitches and French knots (wound once around the needle), according to the colour changes on the chart. Work the pine needles in long stitches using two strands of 700. Work the backstitch stems in the border and the bauble hangers with two strands of 5284. Work all other backstitches using one strand of 310.

3 Once the embroidery is complete, use a contrasting thread, to tack (baste) a stocking outline shape all round the design edges, 1.25cm (½in) out from the red dotted outline shown on the chart.

4 Now make up as a stocking as follows. Place the fusible fleece on the wrong side of the stocking, covering all the tacking (basting) stitches and with an additional 1.25cm (½in) at the top. Press to fuse, according to the manufacturer's directions. Turn the stocking over and cut the top edge seven rows above the tacked line, then cut the remaining stocking shape along the tacked lines. Fold the top edge to the wrong side along the tacked line and press.

5 Cut the backing/lining fabric into two pieces 56 x 46cm (22 x 18in) and with right sides together, place under the stocking and cut to the stocking shape, adding an extra 10cm (4in) at the top. Layer the fabric and stocking as follows: one piece of fabric right side up, the stocking right side up, and the second piece of fabric wrong side up (see diagram). Pin together and stitch a 1.25cm (½in) seam all round, leaving the top edge open and a gap at the bottom for

tucking in the braid. Finish off the raw edges by folding over 1.25cm (½in) to the wrong side and stitching down. Turn the embroidery to the outside, creating a lining and backing. Fold the two top flaps in, aligning them with the folded edge of the embroidery.

The quiet hush
of falling snow,
The candle's light aglow,
The lilt of Christmas carols
That every child will know.
A big old-fashioned Teddy,
Beside the presents bright,
Will bring a peaceful slumber
This silent Christmas night.

6 To make a hanging loop, cut 20cm (8in) of decorative braid, fold it in half and tuck the ends into the left corner of the top edge, in the space between the embroidery and lining. Slipstitch lining and embroidery together at the top edge, catching the cord securely. Using the remaining braid, attach it to the edge of the stocking all round by slipstitching, tucking in the ends neatly at the small opening in the bottom seam. Slipstitch this seam closed to finish.

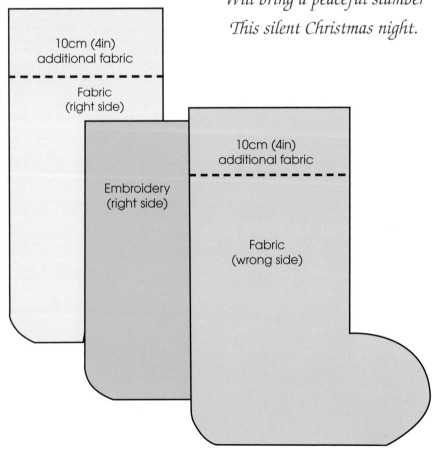

10cm (4in)
additional fabric

Fabric
(right side)

Embroidery
(right side)

10cm (4in)
additional fabric

Fabric
(wrong side)

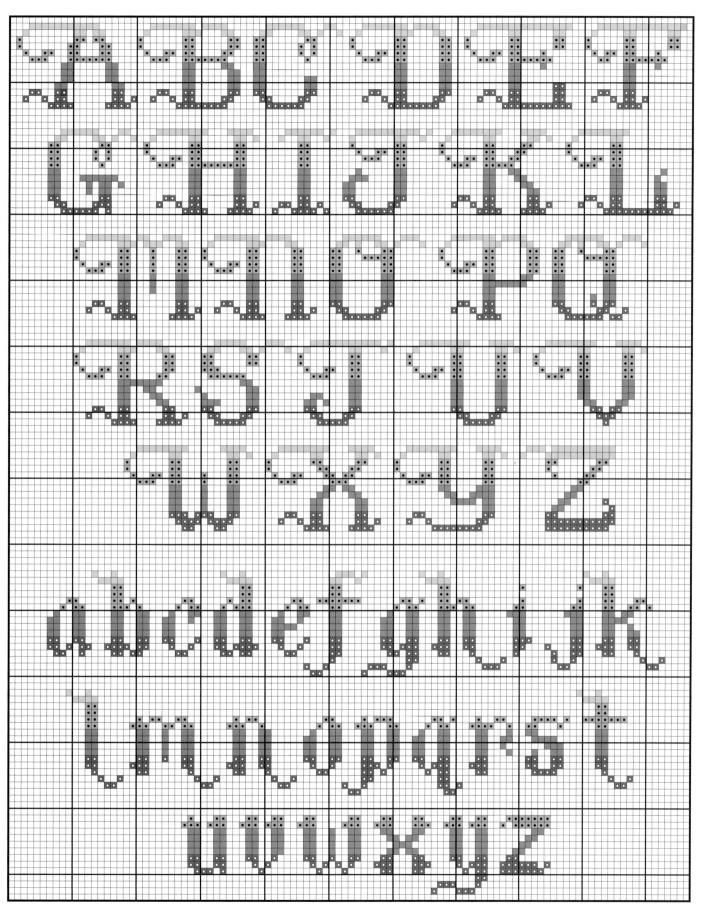

A Victorian Christmas Alphabet Key

DMC stranded cotton
Cross stitch

■ 700　• 702　□ 704　◉ 3818

A Victorian Christmas Key

DMC stranded cotton
Cross stitch

■ 310	∨ 747	
318	− 762	
349	797	
350	∕ 798	
415	799	
598	800	
∕ 676	816	
+ 677	869	
700	898	
• 702	⊤ 945	
704	✕ 951	
725	◉ 3818	
726	∣ 3829	
⊥ 727	∧ 5284	
729	• blanc	

French knots
● 310
● 700
○ 725
● 816
● 5284
○ blanc

Backstitch
—— 310
—— 700
—— 5284

Stocking shape
1.25cm (½in) out
from dotted line

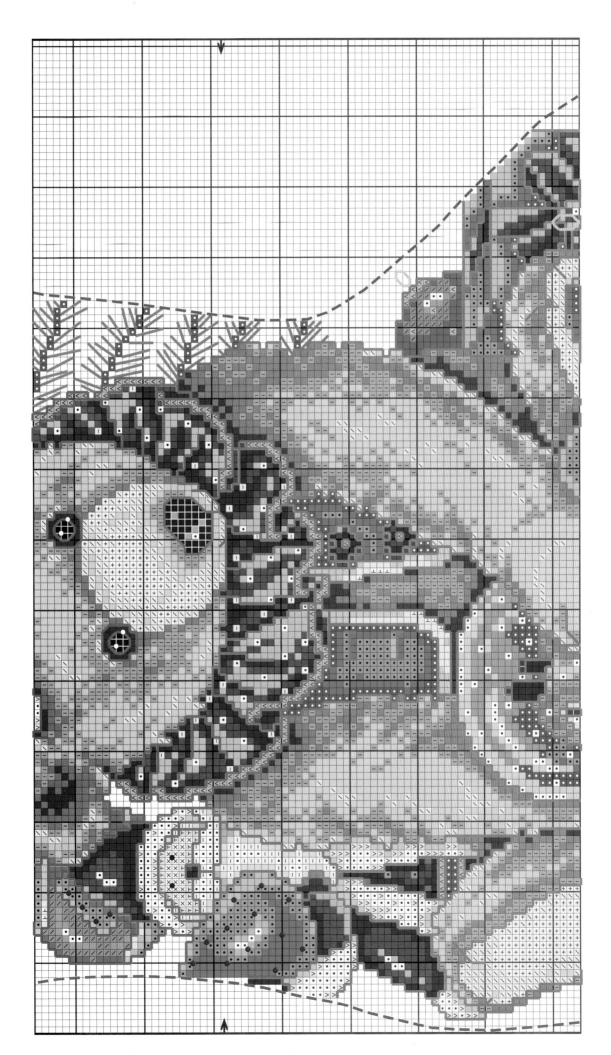

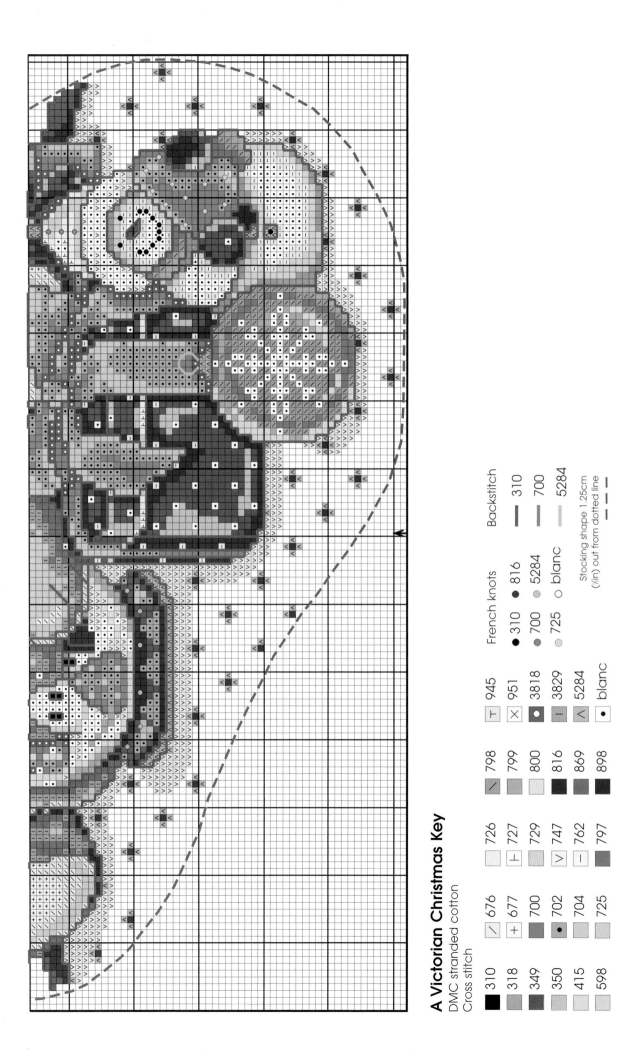

A Victorian Christmas Key

DMC stranded cotton
Cross stitch

■ 310	⁄ 676	⁄ 798	T 945
318	+ 677	799	X 951
349	700	800	▣ 3818
350	• 702	729	– 3829
415	704	∨ 747	⋀ 5284
598	725	– 762	• blanc
		797	816
		898	869
		726	
		727	

French knots
● 310   ● 816
● 700   ● 5284
● 725   ○ blanc

Backstitch
— 310
— 700
— 5284

Stocking shape 1.25cm
(½in) out from dotted line
– – –

Materials, Techniques and Making Up

This brief section describes the materials and equipment required to work the projects, the basic techniques used and some general making up methods. Refer to Suppliers for useful addresses.

MATERIALS

Fabrics The designs have been worked predominantly on a blockweave fabric called Aida. If you change the gauge (count) of the material, that is the number of holes per 2.5cm (1in), then the size of the finished work will alter accordingly. The designs could also be stitched on an evenweave such as linen but will need to be worked over two fabric threads instead of one block.

Threads DMC stranded cotton (floss) has been used for the projects but see Suppliers for other thread companies. The six-stranded skeins can be split into separate strands. The project instructions say how many to use.

Needles Tapestry needles, available in different sizes, are used for cross stitch as they have a rounded point and do not snag fabric.

Frames Whether you use an embroidery frame to keep your fabric taut while stitching is a matter of personal preference. Generally speaking, working with a frame helps to keep the tension even and prevent distortion, while working without a frame is faster and less cumbersome. There are various types on the market – look in your local needlework shop.

TECHNIQUES

Cross stitch embroidery requires few complicated techniques but your stitching will look its best if you follow the simple guidelines below. The projects in the book have been made up in various ways, usually described within the project but some general techniques are covered in Making Up Your Work, beginning on page 107.

Preparing the Fabric

Before starting, check carefully the design size given with each project and make sure that this tallies with the size that you require for your finished embroidery. Make sure that your fabric is at least 5cm (2in) larger all the way round than the finished size of the stitching, to allow for making up. Before beginning to stitch, neaten the edges of the fabric either by hemming or zigzagging to stop the fabric fraying as you work.

Marking the Centre of the Fabric

Regardless of which direction you work the design from it is important to find the centre point of the fabric in order to stitch the work centrally on the fabric. To find the centre, fold the fabric in half horizontally and then vertically, then tack (baste) along the folds (or use tailor's chalk). The centre point is where the two lines of tacking (basting) cross. This point on the fabric should correspond to the centre point on the chart. Remove these tacked or chalk lines on completion of the work.

Using the Charts and Keys

The charts in this book are easy to work from. Each square on the chart represents one stitch. Each coloured square, or coloured square with a symbol, represents a thread colour, with the code number given in the chart key. A few of the designs use fractional stitches (three-quarter and quarter cross stitches) to give more definition. These are shown by half a square (a triangle). Most of the noses, eyes, and open mouths of the bears use three-quarter stitches. Quarter cross stitches are used around the outer edges of the faces and in some of the details in the Alphabet Bears. Solid coloured lines show where backstitches or long stitches are to be worked. French knots are shown by coloured circles.

Each complete chart has arrows at the sides to show the centre point, which you could mark with a pen. Where the charts have been split over several pages, the chart key is repeated. For your own use, you could enlarge and colour photocopy the charts and tape the parts together.

Caring for Embroidery

Several projects are made for repeated use, such as towels, potholders and baby's bibs. You may want to pre-wash the threads you are using to insure colourfastness. Reds, dark colours and bright colours may be of special concern. Before using, wash the floss in a bath of tepid water and mild soap. Rinse well, then lay the floss out flat and dry completely before stitching. Wash completed embroideries in the same way.

To iron work, use a medium setting and cover the ironing board with a thick layer of towelling. Place the stitching right side down and press gently.

Embroideries subject to repeated use and handling, such as potholders, can be backed with a lightweight iron-on interfacing. Simply shape the interfacing to the size of the Aida insert and fuse to the back of the embroidery according to the manufacturer's directions.

Starting and Finishing Stitching

Avoid using knots when starting and finishing as this will make your work lumpy when mounted. Instead, bring the needle up at the start of the first stitch, leaving a 'tail' of about 2.5cm (1in) at the back. Secure the tail in place by working the first few stitches over it. Start new threads by first passing the needle through several stitches on the back of the work.

To finish off thread, pass the needle through some nearby stitches on the wrong side of the work, then cut the thread off, close to the fabric.

Working the Stitches

The embroidery designs in this book predominantly use whole cross stitches. There are also backstitches used to outline parts of the designs and French knots for highlights, particularly for eyes. Some of the designs also use some three-quarter and quarter cross stitches to provide extra detail.

Backstitch

Backstitches are used to give definition to parts of a design and to outline areas. Many of the charts use different coloured backstitches. To work backstitch, follow Fig 1, bringing the needle up at 1 and down at 2. Then bring the needle up again at 3 and down at 4. Keep repeating this pattern of working.

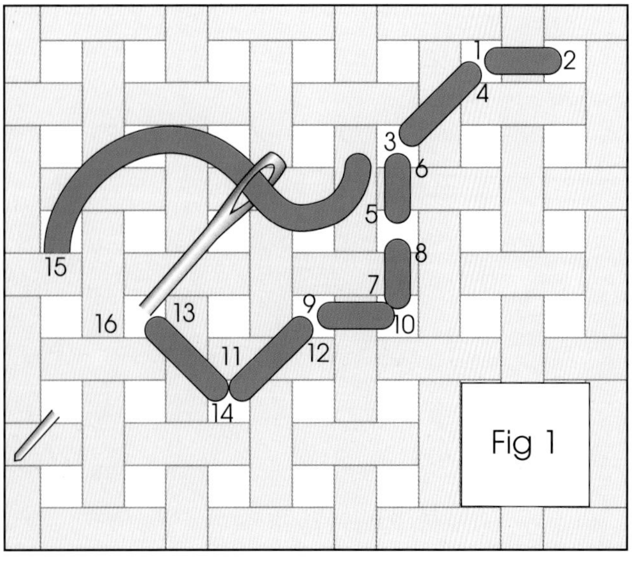

Cross Stitch

A cross stitch has two parts and can be worked in two ways. A complete stitch can be worked singly (Fig 2a) or a number of half cross stitches can be sewn in a line and completed on the return journey (Fig 2b).

To make a cross stitch over a block of Aida, bring the needle up through the fabric at the bottom right-hand side of the stitch (number 1 on Fig 2a) and cross diagonally to the top left-hand corner (2). Push the needle through the hole and bring up through the bottom left-hand corner (3), crossing the fabric diagonally to the top right-hand corner to finish the stitch (4). To work the next stitch, push the needle up through the bottom left-hand corner of the first stitch and repeat the steps above.

To work a line of cross stitches, stitch the first part of the stitch as above and repeat along the row. Complete the crosses on the way back. Note: always finish the cross stitch with the top stitches lying in the same diagonal direction.

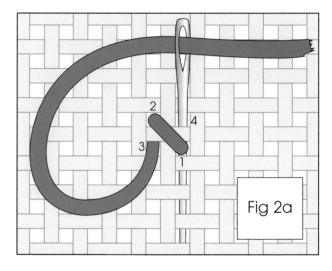

Fig 2a

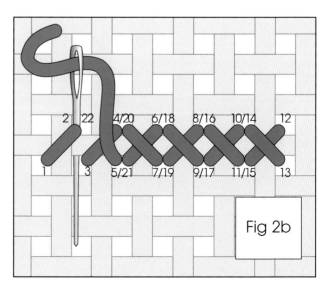

Fig 2b

Fig 1

French Knot

French knots have been used as eye highlights and details in some of the designs, often in various colours. To work, follow Fig 3, bringing the needle and thread up through the fabric at the exact place where the knot is to be positioned. Wrap the thread once or twice around the needle (according to the project instructions), holding the thread firmly and close to the needle. Twist the needle back through the fabric as close as possible to where it first emerged. Holding the knot down carefully, pull the thread through to the back leaving the knot on the surface, securing it with one small stitch on the back.

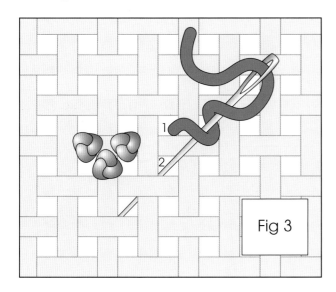

Fig 3

Three-quarter Cross Stitch

Three-quarter cross stitches give more detail to a design. These are shown by a triangle within a square on the chart. To work, make a quarter cross stitch from the corner into the centre of the Aida square, piercing the fabric, and then work a half cross stitch across the other diagonal.

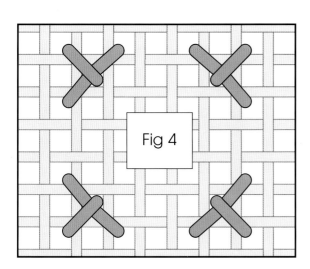

Fig 4

MAKING UP YOUR WORK

The embroideries from this book are very versatile and can be made up in many ways. Generally, making up is included with each project but some general techniques are described here. Metric and imperial measurements have been provided but use one or the other as they are not exactly interchangeable.

Applying Embroidery to a Background Fabric

Sewn method When you have completed stitching the embroidery, use the weave of the Aida fabric as a guide to trim to within twelve rows of the design. Fold over the edges by eight rows, leaving four rows showing around the design. Press into place. Cut a piece of thin cotton wadding (batting) or felt the same size as the design and insert it behind the embroidery before stitching it down. Place the design and wadding on the fabric and machine or hand stitch it in place close to the edge, using the fabric weave as a guide.

Fused method Trim and fold as above and this time use a piece of medium-weight iron-on interfacing behind the embroidery. Use a press cloth to iron and fuse the pieces together from the wrong side, keeping the folded edges in place. Cut a piece of fusible web (I used Steam-a-Seam2 – see Suppliers) the same size as the embroidery. Sandwich the web between the right side of the background fabric and the prepared embroidery, making sure that no edges of web are visible, trimming as necessary. Pin or tack (baste) in place. Using a press cloth, fuse the layers according to the manufacturer's instructions.

Making Up a Book Cover or Photo Album

These instructions show you how to make up the recipe book from Julie's Kitchen and the photograph album from Granny Bear's Memories.

Materials

- One three-ring photo album approximately 25 x 29cm (10 x 11½in)
- 0.5m (½yd) fabric for the outside cover, to tone with the embroidery
- 0.5m (½yd) fabric for the inside covers, to tone with the embroidery
- 0.5m (½yd) white cotton wadding (batting) or felt
- Two 25 x 30cm (10 x 12in) pieces of heavy white card
- 1m (1yd) decorative cording to tone with the embroidery
- 1m (1yd) decorative ribbon to tone with the embroidery
- Spray glue and fabric glue
- One decorative button

1 Measure the inside cover of the album to the fold just before the metal spine. Cut two pieces of heavy card to the measurements, less 1.25cm (½in).

2 Open the binder and lay it flat on the wadding (batting) or felt. Trace the outline of the album on to the batting or felt and cut out. In a well-ventilated area, spray one outside cover of the album with spray glue. Attach the batting or felt and repeat the process for the spine and back cover. Do not pull the felt over the cover too tightly – make sure that the album will close. Trim the edges flush.

3 Lay the open album on the outer cover fabric. Measure and mark 5cm (2in) from all edges and cut the fabric. From the same fabric, cut two strips measuring the length of the metal spine and 7.5cm (3in) wide. Fold over 6mm (¼in) on one long edge of each strip and press. Spray glue on the back of each strip and slide the folded edge under each side of the metal spine. You can use a butter knife to help push the edge beneath the spine.

4 Using the fabric for the inside cover, cut two pieces 1.25cm (½in) larger than the card. Spray glue on one side of each piece of the cut card. Place the fabric on the glued card leaving 1.25cm (½in) of fabric all around. Turn the edges to the back of the card and glue using permanent fabric glue or a hot glue gun.

5 Centre the open album on the outside cover fabric. Turn all the edges to the inside and glue, starting with the centre of each edge, leaving the corners and 7.5cm (3in) from the spine free. Carefully ease the corners to fit, and then glue. At the top and bottom edges by the spine measure the fabric 1.25cm (½in) away from the fold in the album on each side of the metal spine and clip within 1.25cm (½in) of the top edge. Fold the fabric under, between the two cuts, and tuck the folded edge behind the top edge of the metal spine.

6 To assemble the album, cut the ribbon in half and centre one piece on each opening edge of the album at least 5cm (2in) in towards the centre. Carefully glue the back of the covered card. Centre and attach this to the inside covers making sure the fold on the inside of the album is free for closing.

7 Centre the finished embroidery on the cover and glue in place taking care that no glue oozes out from the sides. Draw a thin bead of fabric glue around the edge of the embroidery starting and ending at centre bottom and attach decorative cord. Hide the ends of the cord by gluing on a decorative button.

Making Up into a Card

Many of the designs can be made up as cards. You will need: a ready-made card mount (aperture to fit the embroidery) and craft glue or double-sided tape.

Trim the edges of the embroidery to fit the card. Apply a thin coat of glue or double-sided adhesive tape to the inside of the card opening. Position the embroidery, checking that the stitching is central, and press down firmly. Fold the spare flap inside, sticking in place with glue or tape, and leave to dry before closing.

Decorating a Card Mount You can add a personal touch to ready-made card mounts by attaching buttons, beads, glitter or ribbon with craft glue. You could tie a cord around the inside fold and add a small charm to the end to drape over the outside. Use your creativity to add tiny stars or hearts with coloured markers.

Making Up as a Framed Picture

The designs make wonderful framed pictures. You will need: a picture frame (aperture size to fit embroidery); a piece of plywood or heavyweight card slightly smaller than the frame; and adhesive tape or a staple gun.

Iron your embroidery and trim the edges if necessary, then centre the embroidery on the piece of plywood or card. Fold the edges of the embroidery to the back and use adhesive tape or a staple gun to fix in place. Insert the picture into the frame and secure in place with adhesive tape or staples. For a polished finish, with a wider choice of mounts and frames, take work to a professional framer.

Making a Bolster Cushion Pad

The Teddies on a Roll design has been made up into an attractive bolster cushion. If you cannot find a pad the right size, you can make your own. You will need: two pieces of cotton muslin 91 x 67cm (36 x 26½in); matching sewing thread; heavy button and carpet thread; and 1.12kg (40oz) of polyester stuffing.

Stitch together the 91cm (36in) edges of the muslin with a 1.25cm (½in) seam, forming a fabric tube. Press the seam open. Using heavy button and carpet thread, run two rows of running stitches around each end at 12.5cm (5in) and 6.5cm (2½in) intervals, leaving long ends on the threads for pulling up. Pull and gather the 12.5cm (5in) line of stitches slightly at one end. Begin stuffing, packing evenly and firmly. When you reach the 12.5cm (5in) line of stitches at the other end of the tube, pull and gently gather. Gather the line of stitches at the 6.5cm (2½in) marks, pulling tightly to close each end. Tie off the ends securely. If there is still a bit of an opening at the ends, close it with a few stitches.

Design Works Crafts

My special thanks go to both Susan Goldsmith-Knopp and Daniel Knopp, the owners of Design Works Crafts Inc, for the friendship and the enthusiasm they have shown for my work over the years. Their company has been a leader in the needlework kit industry for the past fourteen years. With a clear vision of what the cross stitch customer is looking for, Design Works Crafts produces fine quality kits that are available at a reasonable price. Distributed world-wide, you can find many of my designs produced by Design Works in the shops in your area, or e-mail them at design_works@msn.com for further information.

Some of the designs included in the book are available in kit form from Design Works Crafts (most assuming making up into framed pictures): Teddies on a Roll #9806; Julie's Kitchen #9638; Baby Bear's Arrival #9642 (called Bear and Bunny Sampler); Granny Bear's Memories #9673 (called Grandchildren); Birthday Bears #352 and #711 (cards); Flower Seed Bear #9809; If you Sprinkle #9423; Beary Merry Christmas (ornaments) #1401 (Angel Bears); #1403 (Happy Holidays and Bear With Wreath) and #1404 (Candy Cane Bear).

Acknowledgments

With heartfelt appreciation, I want to express my thanks to the many people that helped make this book a reality. To all of the staff at Design Works Crafts, thank you for the work you do to bring my designs so wonderfully to kit form. To Donna Richardson, once again, your talent for photography is unerring.

To my stitchers – Bev Ritter, Petie Pickwick, Meem Breyer, Rindy Richards, Lisa Rabon, Judy Trochimiak, Lois Schultz, and Lori West – you were invaluable in bringing my designs to their full beauty. To Judy Suleski, thank you for your dear friendship and unfailing advice. All my love and thanks also to my family for their support and to Earl for his love and his patient ability to share our home with the Teddy Bears for the past eight months.

I want to express my deep appreciation to the many people at David & Charles who helped in the production of this book: Sandra Pruski, Ali Myer, Lisa Forrester and the photographer Lucy Mason – here's to another job well done! Thank you to Cheryl Brown for bringing me the proposal to work on this book and for her continued support. Finally, to Lin Clements, my editor, your friendship and expertise have helped me in so very many ways. Thank you.

www.joanelliottdesign.com

Suppliers

Anne Brinkley Designs Inc
3895B N Oracle Road, Tuscon,
AZ 85705
Tel: 520 888 1462
Fax: 520 888 1483
E-mail: annebrinkleydes@aol.com
A US source for Framecraft products.

Charles Craft, Inc
PO Box 1049
Laurenburg, NC 28353, USA
Tel: 910 844 3521
E-mail: ccraft@carolina.net
Website: www.charlescraft.com
For pre-finished fingertip towels (Park Avenue #6682-2724) and other pre-finished items for the home and baby, and also fabrics for cross stitch. (Coats Crafts UK supply some Charles Craft products in the UK.)

Coats Crafts UK
PO Box 22, Lingfield Estate,
McMullen Road, Darlington,
County Durham DL1 1YQ, UK
Tel: 01325 365457 (for a list of stockists)
For Anchor stranded cotton (floss) and other embroidery supplies. Coats also supply some Charles Craft products.

Design Works Crafts Inc
170 Wilbur Place
Bohemia, NY 11716, USA
Tel: 631 244 5749
Fax: 631 244 6138
Email:customerservice@designworks crafts.com
Website: www.designworkscrafts.com
For cross stitch kits (featuring Joan Elliott designs) and card mounts outside the UK.

DMC Creative World Ltd
Pullman Road, Wigston,
Leicestershire LE18 2DY, UK
Tel: 0116 281 1040
Fax: 0116 281 3592
Website: www.dmc/cw.com
For stranded cotton (floss) and other embroidery supplies.

Framecraft Miniatures Ltd
372–376 Summer Lane, Hockley,
Birmingham B19 3QA, UK
Tel: 0121 212 0551
Fax: 0121 212 0552
Website: www.framecraft.com
For wooden trinket bowls (#W4E) and boxes, notebook covers, pincushions, towels and many other pre-finished items with cross stitch inserts.

Madeira Threads (UK) Ltd
PO Box 6, Thirsk,
North Yorkshire YO7 3YX, UK
Tel: 01845 524880
E-mail: info@madeira.co.uk
Website: www.madeira.co.uk
For Madeira stranded cotton (floss) and other embroidery supplies.

Market Square (Warminster) Ltd
Wing Farm, Longbridge Deverill,
Warminster, Wiltshire BA12 7DD, UK.
Tel: 01985 841041. Fax: 01985 541042
For work boxes and trinket boxes.

Sudberry House
12 Colton Road
East Lyme, CT 06333 USA
Tel: 860 739 6951
E-mail: sales@sudberry.com
Website: www.sudberry.com
For quality wooden products for displaying all forms of needlework, including oval Shaker boxes.

The WARM Company
954 East Union Street,
Seattle, WA 98122, USA
Tel: 1 800 234 WARM
Website: www.warmcompany.com
UK Distributor: W. Williams & Sons Ltd
Tel: 071 263 7311
For fibrefill, cotton wadding (batting), and Steam-A-Seam2 fusible web.

Yarn Tree Designs
PO Box 724
Ames, Iowa 50010-0724, USA
Tel: 1 800 247 3952
E-mail: info@yarntree.com
Website: www.yarntree.com
For large card mounts and a full selection of cross stitch supplies.

Zweigart/Joan Toggit Ltd
262 Old Brunswick Road,
Suite E, Picataway,
NJ 08854-3756, USA
Tel: 732 562 8888
E-mail: info@zweigart.com
Website: www.zweigart.com
For pre-finished table linens and other fabrics for cross stitch.

Index